# THIS BOOK BELONGS TO
## The Library of

..............................................................

..............................................................

©COPYRIGHT2023
**ALL RIGHTS RESERVED**

The content contained within this book may not be reproduced, duplicated, or transmitted without direct written permission from the author or the publisher. Under no circumstances will any blame or legal responsibility be held against the publisher, or author, for any damages, reparation, or monetary loss due to the information contained within this book. Either directly or indirectly.

**Legal Notice:**

This book is copyright protected. This book is only for personal use. You cannot amend, distribute, sell, use, quote, or paraphrase any part, or the content within this book, without the consent of the author or publisher.

**Disclaimer Notice:**

Please note the information contained within this document is for educational and entertainment purposes only. All effort has been executed to present accurate, up-to-date, and reliable, complete information. No warranties of any kind are declared or implied. Readers acknowledge that the author is not engaging in the rendering of legal, financial, medical, or professional advice. The content within this book has been derived from various sources. Please consult a licensed professional before attempting any techniques outlined in this book. By reading this document, the reader agrees that under no circumstances is the author responsible for any losses, direct or indirect, which are incurred as a result of the use of the information contained within this document, including, but not limited to — errors, omissions, or inaccuracies.

Thank you for Purchasing my book and taking the time to read it from front to back. I am always grateful when a reader chooses my work and I hope you enjoyed it!

With the vast selection available online, I am touched that you chose to be purchasing my work and take valuable time out of your life to read it. My hope is that you feel you made the right decision.

I very much would like to know what you thought of the book. Please take the time to write an honest and informative review on Amazon.com. Your experience and opinions will be of great benefit to me and those readers looking to make an informed choice.

**With much thanks.**

# Table of Contents

| | |
|---|---:|
| SUMMARY | 5 |
| Crochet Book Colorful Doilies to Dress Up Your Home | 1 |
|     Pattern Services and Revisions | 26 |
|     Spiderweb | 26 |
|     Give Thanks | 30 |
|     Pink Delight | 35 |
|     Little Fans | 39 |
|     Linen Lace | 42 |
|     Tempest | 46 |
|     Peach Parfait | 50 |
|     Autumn Acorns | 55 |
|     Silver Cones | 58 |
|     Fanfare | 61 |
|     Regency | 65 |
|     Spring Green | 68 |
|     Starflower | 71 |
|     Blue Skies | 74 |
|     Sweetheart | 77 |
|     Mint Julep | 81 |
|     Starburst | 85 |
|     Stitch Guide | 89 |

The Art of Crocheting Doilies is a comprehensive guide that delves into the intricate and beautiful world of doily making through the art of crocheting. This book is a must-have for anyone interested in learning and mastering the techniques required to create stunning doilies.

The book begins by providing a brief history of doilies and their significance in various cultures throughout the world. It explores the origins of doilies and how they have evolved over time, from being purely functional to becoming intricate works of art that are cherished and admired.

The author then delves into the basics of crocheting, providing step-by-step instructions on how to hold the crochet hook, create basic stitches, and read crochet patterns. This section is perfect for beginners who are new to crocheting and want to build a strong foundation before diving into the world of doily making.

Once the basics are covered, the book progresses to more advanced techniques and patterns. It introduces readers to a variety of stitches and techniques that can be used to create different textures, shapes, and designs in doilies. From simple and elegant designs to more complex and intricate patterns, the book offers a wide range of options to suit every skill level and personal preference.

The Art of Crocheting Doilies also provides valuable tips and tricks for troubleshooting common issues that may arise during the crocheting process. Whether it's dealing with tangled yarn, uneven stitches, or understanding complex patterns, the book offers practical solutions and guidance to help readers overcome any obstacles they may encounter.

In addition to the technical aspects of crocheting, the book also explores the creative side of doily making. It discusses color theory, yarn selection, and how to incorporate different embellishments and decorative elements into doilies. This section encourages readers to experiment with their creativity and create unique and personalized doilies that reflect their own style and personality.

The book concludes with a gallery of stunning doily designs created by renowned crocheters from around the world. This serves as both inspiration and motivation for readers to continue honing their skills and exploring new techniques in their doily making journey.

Overall, The Art of Crocheting Doilies is a comprehensive and detailed guide that covers everything from the basics of crocheting to advanced techniques and design principles. It is a valuable resource for both beginners and experienced crocheters alike, providing them with the knowledge and inspiration to create beautiful and intricate doilies that will be cherished for generations to come.

.

Doilies, those delicate and intricate pieces of fabric, have long been associated with a sense of elegance and femininity. Traditionally used as decorative mats or coasters, doilies have evolved over time and have found their place in various aspects of home decor. Their versatility is truly remarkable, as they can be incorporated into different design styles and can serve multiple purposes.

One of the most common uses of doilies in home decor is as table runners or centerpieces. Placed on top of a dining table or a coffee table, doilies instantly add a touch of sophistication and charm to the space. They can be used alone or layered with other fabrics to create a visually appealing arrangement. The intricate patterns and delicate lacework of doilies create a beautiful contrast against the solid surface of the table, making them a focal point of the room.

Doilies can also be used as wall art or wall hangings. When framed or hung on the wall, doilies can transform a plain and boring space into a stunning display of artistry. Their intricate designs and delicate textures add depth and dimension to the walls, creating a unique and visually appealing focal point. Whether used individually or in a group, doilies can be arranged in various patterns and configurations to suit different design aesthetics.

In addition to their decorative uses, doilies can also serve practical purposes in home decor. They can be used as protective covers for furniture, such as armrests or chair backs, to prevent wear and tear. Placing a doily on top of a dresser or a vanity can protect the surface from scratches and spills, while adding a touch of elegance to the furniture piece. Doilies can also be used as decorative accents for pillows or cushions, adding a soft and feminine touch to the overall decor.

Furthermore, doilies can be creatively incorporated into other home decor items. They can be used as lampshade covers, creating a soft and diffused lighting effect in the room. Doilies can also be sewn or glued onto curtains or window treatments, adding a delicate and romantic touch to the windows. Additionally, doilies can be used as decorative elements for vases, candle holders, or even as embellishments for picture frames, giving these everyday objects a unique and personalized touch.

The versatility of doilies in home decor is truly remarkable. From table runners to wall art, from protective covers to decorative accents, doilies can be used in countless ways to enhance the beauty and elegance of any space. Their intricate designs and delicate.

When it comes to crochet, having the right tools and materials is essential for a successful and enjoyable experience. Whether you're a beginner or an experienced crocheter, there are certain items that you simply can't do without.

First and foremost, you'll need a set of crochet hooks. These come in various sizes, ranging from small hooks for delicate projects to larger hooks for bulkier yarns. It's a good idea to invest in a set that includes a range of sizes, as this will allow you to tackle a wide variety of projects. Additionally, consider the material of the hooks - some crocheters prefer metal hooks for their smoothness, while others prefer the grip of wooden or plastic hooks.

Next, you'll need yarn. This is where the fun begins, as there are countless options to choose from. Yarn comes in different weights, which determine the thickness of the yarn. Common weights include lace, fingering, sport, worsted, and bulky. Each weight is suited for different types of projects, so it's important to choose the right one for your intended project. Additionally, consider the fiber content of the yarn - options range from acrylic and cotton to wool and alpaca, each with its own unique characteristics.

To keep track of your progress and count stitches, you'll need stitch markers and a measuring tape. Stitch markers are small, removable markers that can be placed on your work to mark specific stitches or sections. They are especially useful when working in the round or when following complex patterns. A measuring tape is essential for ensuring that your finished project is the correct size and for measuring gauge, which determines how many stitches and rows are needed to achieve a specific size.

Another important tool is a yarn needle or tapestry needle. This needle has a large eye and a blunt tip, making it perfect for weaving in loose ends and sewing pieces together. It's a must-have for finishing off your projects neatly and securely.

Lastly, a crochet project bag or storage case is a great investment for keeping all your tools and materials organized. These bags typically have compartments and pockets to hold your hooks, yarn, and other accessories, making it easy to grab everything you need for your next crochet session.

In conclusion, having the right tools and materials is crucial for successful crochet projects. From crochet hooks and yarn to stitch markers and measuring tape, each item plays a vital role in creating beautiful and functional crochet creations. So, gather your essentials and get ready to embark on a creative

B. Basic Crochet Stitches and Techniques is a comprehensive guide that provides detailed instructions and explanations for beginners who are interested in learning the art of crochet. This resource covers a wide range of basic crochet stitches and techniques, allowing readers to develop a solid foundation in this popular craft.

The book begins by introducing the fundamental tools and materials needed for crochet, including different types of crochet hooks, yarns, and other accessories.

It then delves into the basic crochet stitches, such as the chain stitch, slip stitch, single crochet, double crochet, and treble crochet. Each stitch is explained in a step-by-step manner, accompanied by clear illustrations and diagrams to ensure easy understanding.

In addition to the basic stitches, B. Basic Crochet Stitches and Techniques also covers various techniques that are essential for creating different crochet projects. These techniques include increasing and decreasing stitches, working in the round, changing colors, and joining motifs. The book provides detailed instructions for each technique, along with helpful tips and tricks to make the process smoother and more enjoyable.

Furthermore, this guide goes beyond just teaching the stitches and techniques. It also offers valuable information on reading crochet patterns and charts, understanding gauge and tension, and troubleshooting common crochet problems. This ensures that readers not only learn how to crochet, but also gain the necessary skills to tackle more complex projects in the future.

B. Basic Crochet Stitches and Techniques is written in a clear and concise manner, making it accessible to beginners with no prior crochet experience. The author's passion for crochet shines through in the engaging writing style, making the learning process enjoyable and inspiring. Whether you are looking to create beautiful garments, accessories, or home decor items, this book will equip you with the knowledge and skills needed to bring your crochet projects to life.

Overall, B. Basic Crochet Stitches and Techniques is a must-have resource for anyone interested in learning crochet. With its comprehensive coverage of basic stitches, techniques, and essential crochet knowledge, this book serves as a valuable reference that will empower beginners to embark on their crochet journey with confidence and creativity.

The Yarn Selection Guide is a comprehensive resource that provides detailed information and guidance on selecting the right yarn for your knitting or crochet projects. This guide aims to assist both beginners and experienced crafters in making informed decisions when it comes to choosing the most suitable yarn for their specific needs.

The guide begins by explaining the different types of yarn available in the market, including natural fibers such as cotton, wool, silk, and bamboo, as well as synthetic fibers like acrylic, nylon, and polyester. Each type of yarn is described in detail, highlighting its unique characteristics, advantages, and potential drawbacks. This information allows crafters to understand the properties of each yarn type and make an informed decision based on their project requirements.

Furthermore, the guide provides insights into various yarn weights, which play a crucial role in determining the thickness and drape of the finished project. It explains the standard yarn weight system, ranging from lace weight to super bulky, and provides examples of projects suitable for each weight category. This helps crafters understand which weight is most appropriate for their desired project outcome.

In addition to yarn types and weights, the guide also covers different yarn textures and finishes. It explains the differences between smooth, textured, and novelty yarns, as well as the impact of finishes such as matte, shiny, or metallic. This information allows crafters to consider the visual and tactile effects of the yarn, ensuring that it aligns with their creative vision.

The Yarn Selection Guide also addresses the importance of considering the intended use and care instructions of the finished project. It provides guidance on selecting yarns that are suitable for specific purposes, such as baby items, garments, or home decor. Additionally, it offers tips on how to properly care for different types of yarn, including washing instructions and potential shrinkage or color bleeding concerns.

To further assist crafters in their yarn selection process, the guide includes a glossary of common yarn terms and a list of reputable yarn brands known for their quality and variety. This ensures that crafters have access to reliable resources and can confidently choose yarns that meet their expectations.

Overall, the Yarn Selection Guide is a comprehensive and detailed resource that equips crafters with the knowledge and guidance necessary to make informed decisions when it comes to selecting the right yarn for their knitting or crochet projects. By considering factors such as yarn type, weight, texture, finish, intended use, and care instructions, crafters can ensure that their projects turn out beautifully and meet their desired outcomes.

Understanding yarn weight and fiber is essential for any knitter or crocheter. Yarn weight refers to the thickness or diameter of the yarn strand, which can greatly impact the outcome of your project. It is important to choose the right yarn weight for your desired project, as it can affect the drape, stitch definition, and overall appearance of your finished piece.

Yarn weight is typically categorized into several different categories, ranging from lace weight to super bulky. Lace weight yarn is the thinnest and is often used for delicate and intricate projects such as shawls or doilies. On the other end of the spectrum, super bulky yarn is the thickest and is perfect for cozy and warm projects like blankets or chunky scarves.

Each yarn weight has its own recommended needle or hook size, which can help guide you in selecting the appropriate tools for your project. Using the correct needle or hook size ensures that your stitches are even and consistent, resulting in a more polished and professional-looking finished piece.

In addition to yarn weight, understanding different fiber types is also crucial. Yarn can be made from a variety of materials, including natural fibers like wool, cotton, or silk, as well as synthetic fibers like acrylic or nylon. Each fiber type has its own unique characteristics and properties, which can affect the feel, durability, and care instructions of your finished project.

Natural fibers, such as wool or cotton, are known for their breathability, warmth, and ability to absorb moisture. They are often preferred for garments and accessories that need to be comfortable and regulate body temperature. Synthetic fibers, on the other hand, are often chosen for their affordability, durability, and easy care. They are great for projects that require low maintenance or need to withstand frequent washing.

When selecting yarn for your project, it is important to consider both the yarn weight and fiber type. The pattern you are following may specify a certain yarn weight and fiber, but you can also experiment and substitute with different options to achieve the desired outcome. However, keep in mind that changing the yarn weight or fiber type can affect the gauge and overall size of your project, so it is important to make a gauge swatch and adjust your needle or hook size accordingly.

Overall, understanding yarn weight and fiber is crucial for any knitting or crocheting project. By selecting the right yarn weight and fiber type, you can ensure that your finished piece turns out exactly as you envisioned, with the right drape, stitch definition, and overall.

Round doilies are circular pieces of fabric or lace that are often used as decorative accents for tables or other surfaces. They are typically placed underneath vases, candles, or other decorative items to protect the surface from scratches or heat damage. Round doilies can also be used as standalone decorative pieces, adding a touch of elegance and sophistication to any room.

These doilies come in a variety of sizes, ranging from small ones that are perfect for placing under a teacup or small vase, to larger ones that can be used as centerpieces for dining tables or coffee tables. They are available in a wide range of materials, including cotton, linen, and lace, allowing you to choose the one that best suits your personal style and the overall aesthetic of your space.

Round doilies can be found in various designs and patterns, from simple and understated to intricate and ornate. Some feature delicate floral motifs, while others have geometric patterns or lacework. The choice of design depends on your personal preference and the overall theme or style of your home decor.

In addition to their decorative purposes, round doilies also have practical uses. They can help to absorb moisture and prevent water rings from forming on wooden surfaces, making them ideal for use under glasses or cups. They can also be used to protect delicate or valuable items from scratches or damage when placed on top of them.

Round doilies are versatile and can be used in a variety of settings. They can be used in formal dining rooms, adding a touch of elegance to the table setting. They can also be used in more casual settings, such as on coffee tables or side tables in living rooms or bedrooms. They can even be used outdoors, adding a decorative touch to patio tables or picnic blankets.

Overall, round doilies are a versatile and stylish addition to any home decor. Whether used for their practical purposes or as decorative accents, they add a touch of elegance and sophistication to any space. With their wide range of sizes, materials, and designs, there is a round doily to suit every taste and style.

The output for the input B. Oval Doilies refers to a specific type of doilies known as oval doilies. Doilies are decorative mats or covers, typically made of lace or other delicate materials, that are used to protect surfaces or enhance the aesthetic appeal of furniture, tables, or other items. Oval doilies, as the name suggests, are doilies that are shaped in an oval form.

These oval doilies can come in various sizes, colors, and designs, allowing individuals to choose the one that best suits their preferences and the overall decor of their space. They are often used to add a touch of elegance and sophistication to dining tables, coffee tables, dressers, or any other surface that could benefit from a decorative touch.

The oval shape of these doilies offers a unique and visually appealing alternative to the more common round or square-shaped doilies. The elongated shape of the oval doilies allows them to be used in a variety of ways. They can be placed lengthwise on a table to create a centerpiece or used as a decorative accent on the back of a chair or sofa. The versatility of oval doilies makes them a popular choice for those looking to add a touch of charm and style to their home decor.

In addition to their decorative purposes, oval doilies also serve a functional role. They can protect surfaces from scratches, spills, or heat damage caused by hot dishes or cups. By placing an oval doily under a vase or a candle, for example, you can prevent any potential damage to the surface beneath.

Oval doilies can be made from a variety of materials, including lace, crochet, or even paper. The choice of material can greatly impact the overall look and feel of the doily. Lace oval doilies, for instance, exude a delicate and intricate aesthetic, while crochet oval doilies offer a more rustic and handmade charm. The material used can also affect the durability and maintenance requirements of the doily.

Overall, oval doilies are a versatile and decorative addition to any home or space. They offer a unique shape that adds visual interest and can be used in various ways to enhance the overall aesthetic appeal. Whether used for functional purposes or as a decorative accent, oval doilies are a timeless and elegant choice for those looking to elevate their interior decor.

Traditional lace doilies are delicate and intricate pieces of fabric that are often used as decorative accents in homes. They are typically made from fine threads or yarns, such as cotton or linen, and are crafted using various lace-making techniques. These doilies are known for their intricate patterns and delicate designs, which are created by carefully weaving or crocheting the threads together.

One of the most common types of traditional lace doilies is the crocheted doily. Crocheting involves using a small hook to create loops and stitches, which are then joined together to form the desired pattern. This technique allows for great flexibility and creativity, as crocheters can easily adjust the size and shape of the doily as they work.

Another popular technique used in creating traditional lace doilies is tatting. Tatting involves creating knots and loops using a small shuttle or needle, which are then joined together to form the lace pattern. This technique requires great precision and patience, as the knots and loops must be carefully manipulated to create the desired design.

Traditional lace doilies are often used as decorative accents in homes, particularly on tables, dressers, or mantels. They can add a touch of elegance and sophistication to any room, and are often used to protect surfaces from scratches or stains. These doilies can also be used as decorative elements in other items, such as pillows, curtains, or clothing.

In addition to their decorative purposes, traditional lace doilies also hold cultural and historical significance. They have been used for centuries as a way to showcase the skill and craftsmanship of the maker. In many cultures, lace doilies are passed down through generations as family heirlooms, symbolizing the importance of tradition and heritage.

Overall, traditional lace doilies are beautiful and intricate pieces of fabric that add a touch of elegance and sophistication to any space. Whether used as decorative accents or cherished family heirlooms, these doilies are a testament to the skill and artistry of lace-making techniques.

Modern geometric doilies are a contemporary twist on the traditional doily design. These doilies feature intricate geometric patterns that add a touch of modernity and sophistication to any space. They are perfect for adding a decorative element to tables, shelves, or even walls.

One of the key features of modern geometric doilies is their unique and eye-catching designs. Unlike traditional doilies that often feature floral or lace patterns, these doilies incorporate geometric shapes such as triangles, squares, and hexagons. These shapes are arranged in a symmetrical or asymmetrical manner, creating visually appealing patterns that catch the eye.

Another notable aspect of modern geometric doilies is their versatility. They can be used in a variety of ways to enhance the aesthetic appeal of a room. For instance, they can be placed under vases or decorative objects to create a focal point on a table. They can also be used as wall hangings, adding a touch of texture and visual interest to a plain wall. Additionally, they can be layered on top of each other to create a unique and dynamic look.

In terms of materials, modern geometric doilies are often made from durable and easy-to-clean materials such as cotton or synthetic fibers. This makes them practical for everyday use, as they can be easily washed and maintained. Some doilies may also incorporate other materials such as metallic threads or beads to add a touch of glamour and elegance.

Furthermore, modern geometric doilies are available in a wide range of colors to suit different interior design styles and preferences. They can be found in bold and vibrant hues for a contemporary and eclectic look, or in neutral tones for a more minimalist and understated aesthetic. This variety allows individuals to choose doilies that complement their existing decor or serve as a statement piece in their space.

Overall, modern geometric doilies are a stylish and versatile addition to any home decor. With their intricate designs, durable materials, and wide range of colors, they offer endless possibilities for enhancing the visual appeal of a room. Whether used as table accents, wall hangings, or layered for a unique look, these doilies are sure to make a statement and add a touch of modern elegance to any space.

Overlay crochet is a technique that allows you to create intricate and textured designs on your crochet projects. It involves working additional stitches on top of your base stitches, creating a layered effect that adds depth and dimension to your work.

To start overlay crochet, you will first need to have a solid understanding of basic crochet stitches and techniques. This includes knowing how to create a foundation chain, single crochet, double crochet, and other common stitches. Once you have a good grasp of these fundamentals, you can begin experimenting with overlay crochet.

The key to overlay crochet is understanding how to work the additional stitches on top of your base stitches. This is typically done by inserting your hook into the desired stitch of the previous row or round, and then working the additional stitch around it. This can be done by working a yarn over, inserting your hook into the stitch, and then completing the stitch as you normally would.

One of the main benefits of overlay crochet is the ability to create intricate and detailed designs. By working additional stitches on top of your base stitches, you can create raised motifs, textured patterns, and even three-dimensional effects. This can be especially useful when creating items such as blankets, scarves, or garments, as it adds visual interest and makes your work stand out.

Overlay crochet also allows for a great deal of creativity and customization. You can experiment with different stitch combinations, colors, and textures to create unique and personalized designs. Whether you prefer a more subtle and understated look or a bold and vibrant design, overlay crochet can help you achieve the desired effect.

While overlay crochet can be a bit more challenging than traditional crochet techniques, with practice and patience, you can master this technique and create stunning projects. It is important to take your time and pay attention to the placement of your additional stitches, as this will determine the overall look and texture of your work.

In conclusion, overlay crochet is a technique that allows you to add texture and dimension to your crochet projects. By working additional stitches on top of your base stitches, you can create intricate and detailed designs that make your work stand out. With practice and creativity, you can master this technique and create beautiful and unique crochet pieces.

Blocking and shaping doilies is an essential step in the process of creating these delicate and intricate pieces of crochet or lacework. It involves carefully stretching and shaping the doily to achieve a desired final shape and size, as well as ensuring that the stitches and patterns are well-defined and visually appealing.

The first step in blocking and shaping doilies is to thoroughly wash and clean them. This helps remove any dirt, oils, or other impurities that may have accumulated during the crocheting process. It is important to use a gentle detergent and lukewarm water to avoid damaging the delicate fibers of the doily.

Once the doily is clean, it needs to be carefully stretched and pinned into shape. This is typically done on a blocking board or mat, which provides a stable surface for the doily to be shaped on. The doily is placed on the blocking board and gently stretched and pulled into the desired shape and size.

Pinning is a crucial part of the blocking process. Small stainless steel or rustproof pins are used to secure the doily in place, ensuring that it maintains its shape while drying. The pins are strategically placed along the edges and in the center of the doily, following the pattern and design to ensure that the stitches are evenly stretched and defined.

The doily is left to dry completely in its stretched and pinned position. This can take several hours or even overnight, depending on the size and thickness of the doily. It is important to ensure that the doily is completely dry before removing the pins, as removing them too soon can cause the doily to lose its shape.

Once the doily is dry, the pins can be carefully removed. This should be done with caution to avoid snagging or damaging the delicate fibers of the doily. As the pins are removed, the doily will retain its shape and the stitches will be well-defined and visually appealing.

Blocking and shaping doilies not only enhances their aesthetic appeal but also helps to improve their durability and longevity. By stretching and shaping the doily, the stitches are allowed to settle into their intended positions, creating a more even and balanced finished product. Additionally, blocking helps to remove any uneven tension or puckering that may have occurred during the crocheting process, resulting in a smoother and more professional-looking doily.

In conclusion, blocking and shaping doilies is a crucial step in the creation of these delicate and intricate pieces of crochet or lacework. It involves carefully stretching and shaping the do..

Framing doilies as art is a creative and unique way to showcase these delicate and intricate pieces. Doilies, traditionally used as decorative mats or table covers, are often overlooked as mere functional items. However, by framing them, they can be transformed into stunning works of art that can be displayed and appreciated in a whole new light.

The process of framing doilies involves carefully selecting the doily that will be framed. This can be a vintage doily passed down through generations or a newly crafted one. The doily should have a visually appealing design and be in good condition, as any tears or stains may detract from its overall aesthetic appeal.

Once the doily is chosen, it is important to select a suitable frame that complements its design and size. A frame with a neutral color or a wooden frame can work well, as it allows the doily to take center stage. The frame should also have a deep enough depth to accommodate the thickness of the doily, ensuring that it is not squished or distorted when placed inside.

Before placing the doily in the frame, it is recommended to mount it on a backing board or acid-free matting. This helps to provide support and prevent any sagging or stretching of the doily over time. The backing board or matting should be cut to the exact size of the frame, ensuring a snug fit.

Carefully lay the doily on the backing board or matting, making sure it is centered and positioned as desired. It may be helpful to use small pins or adhesive dots to secure the doily in place, ensuring that it does not shift or move within the frame. Take extra care when handling the doily to avoid any damage or snagging of the delicate threads.

Once the doily is securely in place, gently place the backing board or matting with the doily into the frame. Ensure that it fits properly and that there are no gaps or misalignments. Secure the frame with the provided clips or screws, making sure it is tightly sealed.

Once the doily is framed, it is ready to be displayed. Consider hanging it on a wall as a standalone piece or as part of a gallery wall. Alternatively, it can be placed on a tabletop or shelf, either on its own or alongside other decorative items. The framed doily can add a touch of elegance and nostalgia to any space, creating a focal point that sparks conversation and admiration.

One of the key challenges in the manufacturing process is preventing warping and curling of the final product. Warping refers to the distortion or bending of a material, while curling refers to the tendency of a material to curl or roll up at the edges. Both warping and curling can significantly affect the quality and functionality of the product, making it essential to address these issues.

There are several factors that contribute to warping and curling, including the inherent properties of the material, the manufacturing process, and external factors such as temperature and humidity. Understanding these factors is crucial in developing effective strategies to prevent warping and curling.

The choice of material plays a significant role in determining the susceptibility to warping and curling. Different materials have varying levels of dimensional stability, which refers to their ability to maintain their shape and size under different conditions. Materials with low dimensional stability, such as certain types of plastics or wood, are more prone to warping and curling. On the other hand, materials with high dimensional stability, such as metals or certain composites, are less likely to experience these issues.

# Spiderweb

## SKILL LEVEL

INTERMEDIATE

## FINISHED SIZE
12 inches square

## MATERIALS
- Aunt Lydia's Classic size 10 crochet cotton (350 yds per ball):
  1 ball natural
- Size 7/1.65mm steel crochet hook or size needed to obtain gauge

## GAUGE
6 sts and 5 ch-1 sps = 1 inch; 4 rows = 1 inch

## SPECIAL STITCH
**Picot:** Ch 3, sl st in top of last st made.

## INSTRUCTIONS
### DOILY
**Row 1:** Ch 47, dc in 3rd ch from hook *(first 2 chs do not count as dc)*, [ch 1, sk next ch, dc in next ch] across, turn. *(23 dc, 22 ch sps)*

**Rows 2–18:** Ch 4 *(counts as first dc and ch-1 sp)*, dc in next st, [ch 1, dc in next st] across, turn.

**Rnd 19:** Working in rnds, sl st in first ch sp, ch 3, 8 dc in same ch sp *(corner)*, ch 2, sk next st and next ch sp, sc in next ch sp, ch 2, sk next st, [dc in next ch sp, dc in next st] 15 times, dc in next ch sp, ch 2, sk next st, sc in next ch sp, ch 2, sk next st, next ch sp and next st, 9 dc in last ch sp *(corner)*, working in ends of rows, ch 2, sk first row, sc in next row, ch 2, evenly sp 30 dc in end of next 13 rows, ch 2, sc in next row, ch 2, sk next row, working in starting ch across row 1, 9 dc in ch sp at corner, ch 2, sk next ch sp, sc in next ch sp, ch 2, sk next ch at bottom of st, [dc in next ch sp, dc in next ch at bottom of st] 15 times, dc in next ch sp, ch 2, sk next ch sp and next ch, sc in next ch sp, ch 2, sk next ch sp and next ch, 9 dc in corner ch sp, working in ends of rows, ch 2, sk first 2 rows, sc in next row, ch 2, evenly sp 30 dc in end of next 13 rows, ch 2, sc in next row, ch 2, sk next 2 rows, join with sl st in 3rd ch of beg ch-3.

**Rnd 20:** Ch 4, *dc in next dc, [ch 1, dc in next dc] 7 times, ch 2, sk next 2 ch sps and first dc of next group, dc in each dc across group leaving last dc unworked, ch 2, sk next 2 ch sps**, dc in next dc, rep from * around, ending last rep at **, join with sl st in 3rd ch of beg ch-4.

**Rnd 21:** Ch 5 *(counts as first dc and ch-2 sp)*, *dc in next dc, [ch 2, dc in next dc] 7 times, ch 3, sk next ch sp and first dc of next group, dc in each dc across group leaving last dc unworked, ch 3, sk next ch sp**, dc in next dc, rep from * around, ending last rep at **, join with sl st in 3rd ch of beg ch-5.

**Rnd 22:** Ch 6 *(counts as first dc and ch-3 sp)*, *dc in next dc, [ch 3, dc in next dc] 7 times, ch 4, sk next ch sp and first dc of next group, dc in each dc across group leaving last dc unworked, ch 4, sk next ch sp**, dc in next dc, rep from * around, ending last rep at **, join with sl st in 3rd ch of beg ch-6.

**Rnd 23:** Ch 7 *(counts as first dc and ch-4 sp)*, *dc in next dc, [ch 4, dc in next dc] 7 times, ch 5, sk next ch sp and first dc of next group, dc in each dc across group leaving last dc unworked, ch 5, sk next ch sp**, dc in next dc, rep from * around, ending last rep at **, join with sl st in 3rd ch of beg ch-7.

**Rnd 24:** Ch 8 *(counts as first dc and ch-5 sp)*, *dc in next dc, [ch 5, dc in next dc] 7 times, ch 6, sk next ch sp and first dc of next group, dc in each dc across group leaving last dc unworked, ch 6, sk next ch sp**, dc in next dc, rep from * around, ending last rep at **, join with sl st in 3rd ch of beg ch-8.

**Rnd 25:** Ch 9 *(counts as first dc and ch-6 sp)*, *dc in next dc, [ch 6, dc in next dc] 7 times, ch 7, sk next ch sp and first dc of next group, dc in each dc across group leaving last dc unworked, ch 7, sk next ch sp**, dc in next dc, rep from * around, ending last rep at **, join with sl st in 3rd ch of beg ch-9.

**Rnds 26–29:** Ch 9 *(counts as first dc and ch-6 sp)*, *dc in next dc, [ch 6, dc in next dc] 7 times, ch 7, sk next ch sp and first dc of next group, dc in each dc across group leaving last dc unworked, ch 7, sk next ch sp**, dc in next dc, rep from * around, ending last rep at **, join with sl st in 3rd ch of beg ch-9.

**Rnd 30:** Ch 10 *(counts as first dc and ch-7 sp)*, *dc in next dc, [ch 7, dc in next dc] 7 times, ch 9, sk next ch sp and first dc of next group, dc in each dc across group leaving last dc unworked, ch 9, sk next ch sp**, dc in next dc, rep from * around, ending last rep at **, join with sl st in 3rd ch of beg ch-10.

**Rnd 31:** Ch 10 *(counts as first dc and ch-7 sp)*, *dc in next dc, [ch 7, dc in next dc] 7 times, ch 10, sk next ch sp and first dc of next group, dc in each dc across group leaving last dc unworked, ch 10, sk next ch sp**, dc in next dc, rep from * around, ending last rep at **, join with sl st in 3rd ch of beg ch-10.

**Rnd 32:** Ch 11 *(counts as first dc and ch-8 sp)*, *dc in next dc, [ch 8, dc in next dc] 7 times, ch 10, sk next ch sp and first dc of next group, dc in each dc across group leaving last dc unworked, ch 10, sk next ch sp**, dc in next dc, rep from * around, ending last rep at **, join with sl st in 3rd ch of beg ch-11.

**Rnd 33:** Ch 11 *(counts as first dc and ch-8 sp)*, *dc in next dc, [ch 8, dc in next dc] 7 times, ch 10, sk next ch sp and first dc of next group, dc in each dc across group leaving last dc unworked, ch 10, sk next ch sp**, dc in next dc, rep from * around, ending last rep at **, join with sl st in 3rd ch of beg ch-11.

**Rnd 34:** Ch 1, (6 sc, **picot**—*see Special Stitch*, 6 sc) in each of first 9 ch sps, *sc in each of next 2 dc**, (6 sc, picot, 6 sc) in each of next 10 ch sps, rep from * around, ending last rep at **, (6 sc, picot, 6 sc) in last ch sp, join with sl st beg sc. Fasten off.

# Give Thanks

## SKILL LEVEL

INTERMEDIATE

## FINISHED SIZE
14 inches in diameter

## MATERIALS
- Aunt Lydia's Classic size 10 crochet cotton (350 yds per ball): 1 ball #431 pumpkin
- Size 7/1.65mm steel crochet hook or size needed to obtain gauge

## GAUGE
Rnds 1–3 = 2 inches in diameter

## SPECIAL STITCHES
**Shell:** (2 tr, ch 2, 2 tr) in next ch sp.
**Picot:** Ch 3, sl st in 3rd ch from hook.

## INSTRUCTIONS

### DOILY

**Rnd 1:** Ch 6, sl st in first ch to form ring, ch 1, 12 sc in ring, join with sl st in beg sc.

**Rnd 2:** Ch 1, sc in first st, [ch 12, sc in next st] around, join with ch 6, dtr in beg sc, forming last ch sp.

**Rnd 3:** Ch 1, sc in ch sp just made, ch 5, [sc in next ch sp, ch 5] around, join with sl st in beg sc.

**Rnd 4:** Sl st in each of first 2 chs, ch 1, sc in same ch sp, ch 6, [sc in next ch sp, ch 6] around, join with sl st in beg sc.

**Rnd 5:** Sl st in each of first 2 chs, ch 1, sc in same ch sp, *ch 6, **shell** *(see Special Stitches)* in next ch sp, ch 6**, sc in next ch sp, rep from * around, ending last rep at **, join with sl st in beg sc.

**Rnd 6:** Sl st in each of first 2 chs, ch 1, sc in same ch sp, *ch 6, shell in ch sp of next shell**, [ch 6, sc in next ch sp] twice, rep from * around, ending last rep at **, ch 6, sc in last ch sp, ch 6, join with sl st in beg sc.

**Rnd 7:** Sl st in each of first 2 chs, ch 1, sc in same ch, *ch 6, shell**, [ch 6, sc in next ch sp] 3 times, rep from * around, ending last rep at **, [ch 6, sc in next ch sp] twice, ch 6, join with sl st in beg sc.

**Rnd 8:** Sl st in each of first 2 chs, ch 1, sc in same ch, *ch 6, shell**, [ch 6, sc in next ch sp] 4 times, rep from * around, ending last rep at **, [ch 6, sc in next ch sp] 3 times, ch 6, join with sl st in beg sc.

**Rnd 9:** Sl st in each of first 2 chs, ch 1, sc in same ch, *ch 6, shell, [ch 6, sc in next ch sp] twice, ch 6, shell, ch 6**, [sc in next ch sp, ch 6] twice, rep from * around, ending last rep at **, sc in last ch sp, ch 6, join with sl st in beg sc.

**Rnd 10:** Sl st in each of first 2 chs, ch 1, sc in same ch, *ch 6, (shell, ch 2, 2 tr) in next shell, [ch 6, sc in next ch sp] 3 times, ch 3, (sc, ch 5, sc) in ch sp of next shell, ch 3, [sc in next ch sp, ch 6] twice**, sc in next ch sp, rep from * around, ending last rep at **, join with sl st in beg sc.

**Rnd 11:** Sl st in each of first 2 chs, ch 1, sc in same ch, *ch 6, shell, ch 2, shell, ch 6, sc in next ch sp, [ch 4, sc in next ch sp] twice, ch 4, 9 tr in next ch-5 sp**, [ch 4, sc in next ch sp] 3 times, rep from * around, ending last rep at **, [ch 4, sc in next ch sp] twice, ch 4, join with sl st in beg sc.

**Rnd 12:** Sl st in each of first 2 chs, ch 1, sc in same ch, *ch 6, shell, ch 2, 2 tr in next ch sp, ch 2, shell, ch 6, sc in next ch sp, [ch 4, sc in next ch sp] twice, ch 4, sk next ch sp, sc in next tr, [ch 2, sc in next tr] 8 times, ch 4, sk next ch sp, [sc in next ch sp, ch 4] twice**, sc in next ch sp, rep from * around, ending last rep at **, join with sl st in beg sc.

**Rnd 13:** Sl st in each of first 2 chs, ch 1, sc in same ch sp, *ch 6, (tr, ch 2, tr) in ch sp of next shell, ch 4, sc in next ch sp, ch 6, sc in next ch sp, ch 4, (tr, ch 2, tr) in ch sp of next shell, ch 6, [sc in next ch sp, ch 4] 3 times, sk next ch sp, sc in next ch-2 sp, [ch 2, sc in next ch-2 sp] 7 times, ch 4, sk next ch sp, [sc in next ch sp, ch 4] twice**, sc in next ch sp, rep from * around, ending last rep at **, join with sl st in beg sc.

**Rnd 14:** Sl st in each of first 2 chs, ch 1, sc in same ch sp, *ch 6, (tr, ch 2, tr) in next ch sp, ch 4, sc in next ch sp, ch 4, 7 dc in next ch-6 sp, ch 4, sc in next ch sp, ch 4, (tr, ch 2, tr) in next ch sp, ch 6, [sc in next ch sp, ch 4] 3 times, sk next ch sp, sc in next ch-2 sp, [ch 2, sc in next ch-2 sp] 6 times, ch 4, sk next ch sp, [sc in next ch sp, ch 4] twice**, sc in next ch sp, rep from * around, ending last rep at **, join with sl st in beg sc.

**Rnd 15:** Sl st in each of first 2 chs, ch 1, sc in same ch sp, *ch 6, (tr, ch 2, tr) in next ch sp, ch 4, sc in next ch sp, ch 2, sk next ch sp, sc in next dc, [ch 2, sc in next dc] 6 times, ch 2, sk next ch sp, sc in next ch sp, ch 4, (tr, ch 2, tr) in next ch sp, ch 6, [sc in next ch sp, ch 4] 3 times, sk next ch sp, sc in next ch-2 sp, [ch 2, sc in next ch-2 sp] 5 times, ch 4, sk next ch sp, [sc in next ch sp, ch 4] twice**, sc in next ch sp, rep from * around, ending last rep at **, join with sl st in beg sc.

**Rnd 16:** Sl st in each of first 2 chs, ch 1, sc in same ch sp, *ch 6, (tr, ch 2, tr) in next ch sp, ch 4, sc in next ch sp, ch 3, sk next ch sp, sc in next ch-2 sp, [ch 2, sc in next ch-2 sp] 5 times, ch 3, sk next ch sp, sc in next ch sp, ch 4, (tr, ch 2, tr) in next ch sp, ch 6, [sc in next ch sp, ch 4] 3 times, sk next ch sp, sc in next ch-2 sp, [ch 2, sc in next ch-2 sp] 4 times, ch 4, sk next ch sp, [sc in next ch sp, ch 4] twice**, sc in next ch sp, rep from * around, ending last rep at **, join with sl st in beg sc.

**Rnd 17:** Sl st in each of first 2 chs, ch 1, sc in same ch sp, *ch 6, (tr, ch 2, tr) in next ch sp, ch 4, sc in next ch sp, ch 4, sk next ch sp, sc in next ch-2 sp, [ch 2, sc in next ch-2 sp] 4 times, ch 4, sk next ch sp, sc in next ch sp, ch 4, (tr, ch 2, tr) in next ch sp, ch 6, [sc in next ch sp, ch 4] 3 times, sk next ch sp, sc in next ch-2 sp, [ch 2, sc in next ch-2 sp] 3 times, ch 4, sk next ch sp, [sc in next ch sp, ch 4] twice**, sc in next ch sp, rep from * around, ending last rep at **, join with sl st in beg sc.

**Rnd 18:** Sl st in each of first 2 chs, ch 1, sc in same ch sp, *ch 6, (3 tr, ch 2, 3 tr) in next ch sp, ch 4, sc in next ch sp, ch 4, sk next ch sp, sc in next ch-2 sp, [ch 2, sc in next ch-2 sp] 3 times, ch 4, sk next ch sp, sc in next ch sp, ch 4, (3 tr, ch 2, 3 tr) in next ch sp, ch 6, [sc in next ch sp, ch 4] 3 times, sk next ch sp, sc in next ch-2 sp, [ch 2, sc in next ch-2 sp] twice, ch 4, sk next ch sp, [sc in next ch sp, ch 4] twice**, sc in next ch sp, rep from * around, ending last rep at **, join with sl st in beg sc.

**Rnd 19:** Sl st in each of first 2 chs, ch 1, sc in same ch sp, *ch 6, ({2 tr, ch 2} twice, 2 tr) in next ch sp, ch 4, sc in next ch sp, ch 4, sk next ch sp, sc in next ch-2 sp, [ch 2, sc in next ch-2 sp] twice, ch 4, sk next ch sp, sc in next ch sp, ch 4, ({2 tr, ch 2} twice, 2 tr) in next ch sp, ch 6, [sc in next ch sp, ch 4] 3 times, sk next ch sp, sc in next ch-2 sp, ch 2, sc in next ch-2 sp, ch 4, sk next ch sp, [sc in next ch sp, ch 4] twice**, sc in next ch sp, rep from * around, ending last rep at **, join with sl st in beg sc.

**Rnd 20:** Sl st in each of first 2 chs, ch 1, sc in same ch sp, *ch 6, shell, ch 2, shell, ch 4, sc in next ch sp, ch 4, sk next ch sp, sc in next ch-2 sp, ch 2, sc in next ch-2 sp, ch 4, sk next ch sp, sc in next ch sp, ch 4, shell, ch 2, shell, ch 6, [sc in next ch sp, ch 4] twice, sc in next ch sp, ch 5, sk next ch sp, sc in next ch-2 sp, ch 5, sk next ch sp, [sc in next ch sp, ch 4] twice**, sc in next ch sp, rep from * around, ending last rep at **, join with sl st in beg sc.

**Rnd 21:** Sl st in each of first 2 chs, ch 1, sc in same ch sp, *ch 6, shell, ch 2, 2 tr in next ch sp, ch 2, shell, ch 4, sc in next ch sp, ch 5, sk next ch sp, sc in next ch-2 sp, ch 5, sk next ch sp, sc in next ch sp, ch 4, shell, ch 2, 2 tr in next ch sp, ch 2, shell, ch 6, [sc in next ch sp, ch 4] twice, sc in next ch sp, ch 3, (tr, ch 1, tr) in next ch sp, ch 1, (tr, ch 1, tr) in next ch sp, ch 3, [sc in next ch sp, ch 4] twice**, sc in next ch sp, rep from * around, ending last rep at **, join with sl st in beg sc.

**Rnd 22:** Sl st in each of first 2 chs, ch 1, sc in same ch sp, *ch 6, (3 tr, ch 2, 3 tr) in ch sp of next shell, [ch 3, sc in next ch sp] twice, ch 3, (3 tr, ch 2, 3 tr) in ch sp of next shell, [ch 4, sc in next ch sp] twice, ch 3, [sc in next ch sp, ch 4] twice, (3 tr, ch 2, 3 tr) in ch sp of next shell, [ch 3, sc in next ch sp] twice, ch 3, (3 tr, ch 2, 3 tr) in ch sp of next shell, ch 6, [sc in next ch sp, ch 4] twice, sc in next ch sp, ch 5, sk next 2 ch sps, sc in next ch sp, ch 5, sk next 2 ch sps, [sc in next ch sp, ch 4] twice**, sc in next ch sp, rep from * around, ending last rep at **, join with sl st in beg sc.

**Rnd 23:** Ch 1, sc in each st around with (sc, **picot**—*see Special Stitches*, sc) in each ch-2 sp, (2 sc, picot, 2 sc) in each ch-4 sp and (3 sc, picot, 3 sc) in each ch-6 sp, join with sl st in beg sc. Fasten off.

# Pink Delight

## SKILL LEVEL
INTERMEDIATE

## FINISHED SIZE
10½ inches square

## MATERIALS
- Size 10 crochet cotton:
    300 yds pink
- Size 7/1.65mm steel hook or size needed to obtain gauge

## GAUGE
Rnds 1 and 2 = 1½ inches in diameter

## SPECIAL STITCHES

**Cluster (cl):** Holding last lp of each st on hook, 3 tr in next ch sp, yo, pull through all lps on hook.

**Picot:** Ch 3, sl st in last st made.

## INSTRUCTIONS

### DOILY

**Rnd 1:** Ch 6, sl st in first ch to form ring, ch 4 *(counts as first tr)*, 3 tr in ring, ch 3, [4 tr in ring, ch 3] 3 times, join with sl st in 4th ch of beg ch-4. *(16 tr)*

**Rnd 2:** Ch 4, tr in each of next 3 sts, *ch 4, sc in next ch sp, ch 4**, tr in each of next 4 sts, rep from * around, ending last rep at **, join with sl st in 4th ch of beg ch-4.

**Rnd 3:** Ch 4, tr in each of next 3 sts, *[ch 4, sc in next ch sp] twice, ch 4**, tr in each of next 4 sts, rep from * around, ending last rep at **, join with sl st in 4th ch of beg ch-4.

**Rnd 4:** Ch 4, tr in each of next 3 sts, *ch 4, sc in next ch sp, ch 4, (tr, ch 2, tr) in next ch sp, ch 4, sc in next ch sp, ch 4**, tr in each of next 4 sts, rep from * around, ending last rep at **, join with sl st in 4th ch of beg ch-4.

**Rnd 5:** Sl st in next st, ch 5 *(counts as first tr and ch-1 sp)*, tr in next st, *ch 4, sk next st, sc in next ch sp, ch 4, sk next ch sp, (2 tr, ch 2, 2 tr) in next ch sp, ch 4, sk next ch sp, sc in next ch sp, ch 4**, sk next st, tr in next st, ch 2, tr in next st, rep from * around, ending last rep at **, join with sl st in 4th ch of beg ch-4.

**Rnd 6:** Sl st in first ch sp, ch 4, (tr, ch 2, 2 tr) in same ch sp, *[ch 4, sc in next ch sp] twice, ch 4, (3 tr, ch 2, 3 tr) in next ch sp, ch 4, [sc in next ch sp, ch 4] twice**, (2 tr, ch 2, 2 tr) in next ch sp, rep from * around, ending last rep at **, join with sl st in 4th ch of beg ch-4.

**Rnd 7:** Sl st across to first ch sp, ch 4, (2 tr, ch 2, 3 tr) in same ch sp, *[ch 4, sc in next ch sp] 3 times, ch 4, ({2 tr, ch 2} twice, 2 tr) in next ch sp, ch 4, [sc in next ch sp, ch 4] 3 times**, (3 tr, ch 2, 3 tr) in next ch sp, rep from * around, ending last rep at **, join with sl st in 4th ch of beg ch-4.

**Rnd 8:** Sl st across to first ch sp, ch 4, (tr, {ch 2, 2 tr} twice) in same ch sp, *[ch 4, sc in next ch sp] 4 times, ch 4, [tr in each of next 2 sts, ch 3, sk next ch sp] twice, tr in each of next 2 sts, ch 4, [sc in next ch sp, ch 4] 4 times**, ({2 tr, ch 2} twice, 2 tr) in next ch sp, rep from * around, ending last rep at **, join with sl st in 4th ch of beg ch-4.

**Rnd 9:** Ch 4, tr in next st, *[ch 3, sk next ch sp, tr in each of next 2 sts] twice, [ch 4, sc in next ch sp] 5 times, ch 4, (**cl**—*see Special Stitches*, ch 2, cl) in next ch sp, ch 2, (cl, ch 2, cl) in next ch sp, ch 4, [sc in next ch sp, ch 4] 5 times**, tr in each of next 2 sts, rep from * around, ending last rep at **, join with sl st in 4th ch of beg ch-4.

**Row 10:** Ch 5, tr in next st, *[ch 1, (tr, ch 1, tr) in next ch sp, tr in next st, ch 1, tr in next st] twice, [ch 4, sc in next ch sp] 6 times, ch 4, (cl, ch 2, cl) in next ch sp, ch 4, sc in next ch sp, ch 4, (cl, ch 2, cl) in next ch sp, ch 4, [sc in next ch sp, ch 4] 6 times**, tr in next st, ch 1, tr in next st, rep from * around, ending last rep at **, join with sl st in 4th ch of beg ch-5.

**Rnd 11:** Ch 6 *(counts as first tr and ch-2 sp)*, *tr in next st, [ch 2, tr in next st] 8 times, [ch 4, sc in next ch sp] 3 times, ch 3, cl in next ch sp, ch 3, [sc in next ch sp, ch 4] 3 times, cl in next ch sp, [ch 4, sc in next ch sp] twice, ch 4, cl in next ch sp, [ch 4, sc in next ch sp] 3 times, ch 3, in next ch sp, ch 3, [sc in next ch sp, ch 4] 3 times, cl in next ch sp, ch 3, [sc in next ch sp, ch 4] 3 times**, tr in next st, ch 2, rep from * around, ending last rep at **, join with sl st 4th ch of beg ch-6.

**Rnd 12:** Ch 7 *(counts as first tr and ch-3 sp)*, *tr in next st, [ch 3, tr in next st] 8 times, [ch 4, sc in next ch sp] 3 times, ch 3, cl in next ch sp, ch 2, cl in next ch sp, ch 3, [sc in next ch sp, ch 4] 4 times, (tr, ch 1, tr) in next ch sp, [ch 4, sc in next ch sp] 4 times, ch 3, cl in next ch sp, ch 2, cl in next ch sp, ch 3, [sc in next ch sp, ch 4] 3 times**, tr in next st, ch 3, rep from * around, ending last rep at **, join with sl st 4th ch of beg ch-6.

**Rnd 13:** Ch 8 *(counts as first tr and ch-4 sp)*, *tr in next st, [ch 4, tr in next st] 8 times, [ch 4, sc in next ch sp] twice, ch 4, sk next 2 ch sps, cl in next ch sp, ch 4, sk next 2 ch sps, [sc in next ch sp, ch 4] twice, sk next ch sp, (2 tr, ch 3, 2 tr) in next ch sp, ch 4, sk next ch sp, [sc in next ch sp, ch 4] twice, sk next 2 ch sps, cl in next ch sp, ch 4, sk next 2 ch sps, [sc in next ch sp, ch 4] twice**, tr in next st, ch 4, rep from * around, ending last rep at **, join with sl st 4th ch of beg ch-6.

**Rnd 14:** Sl st in first ch sp, ch 1, (sc, **picot**—*see Special Stitches*, sc, ch 3) in same ch sp and in each ch sp around, join with sl st in beg sc. Fasten off.

# Little Fans

## SKILL LEVEL
INTERMEDIATE

## FINISHED SIZE
5½ inches square

## MATERIALS
- DMC Cebelia size 10 crochet cotton (282 yds per ball):
   1 ball #747 sea mist blue
- Size 7/1.65mm steel hook or size needed to obtain gauge

## GAUGE
Rnds 1 and 2 = 1 inch in diameter

## INSTRUCTIONS

## DOILY

**Rnd 1:** Ch 5, sl st in first ch to form ring, ch 3 *(counts as first dc)* 2 dc in ring, ch 2, [3 dc in ring, ch 2] 3 times, join with sl st in 3rd ch of beg ch-3. *(12 dc)*

**Rnd 2:** Ch 3, dc in each dc around with (2 dc, ch 2, 2 dc) in each ch sp, join with sl st in 3rd ch of beg ch-3. *(28 dc)*

**Rnd 3:** Ch 3, dc in each dc around with (2 dc, ch 2, 2 dc) in each ch sp, join with sl st in 3rd ch of beg ch-3. *(44 dc)*

**Rnd 4:** Sl st in next st, ch 4 *(counts as first dc and ch-1 sp)*, *sk next st, [dc in next st, ch 1, sk next st] across** to next ch sp, 6 dc in ch sp, ch 1, rep from * around, ending last rep at **, join with sl st in 3rd ch of beg ch-4.

**Rnd 5:** Ch 4, skipping ch sps, [dc in next st, ch 1] twice, *2 dc in each of next 6 sts, ch 1**, [dc in next st, ch 1] 5 times, rep from * around, ending last rep at **, [dc in next st, ch 1] across, join with sl st in 3rd ch of beg ch-4.

**Rnd 6:** Ch 4, skipping ch sps, [dc in next st, ch 1] twice, *dc in next st, [ch 1, dc in next st] 11 times, ch 1**, [dc in next st, ch 1] 5 times, rep from * around, ending last rep at **, [dc in next st, ch 1] across, join with sl st in 3rd ch of beg ch-4.

**Rnd 7:** Ch 3, [dc in next ch sp, dc in next st] twice, *ch 2, sk next ch sp, dc in next st, [ch 1, dc in next st] 11 times, ch 2, sk next ch sp**, [dc in next st, dc in next ch sp] 4 times, dc in next st, rep from * around, ending last rep at **, [dc in next st, dc in next ch sp] across, join with sl st in 3rd ch of beg ch-3.

**Rnd 8:** Ch 3, dc in each of next 3 sts, *ch 3, sk next st and next ch sp, dc in next st, [ch 1, dc in next st] 11 times, ch 3, sk next ch sp and next st**, dc in each of next 7 sts, rep from * around, ending last rep at **, dc in each st across, join with sl st in 3rd ch of beg ch-3.

**Rnd 9:** Ch 3, dc in each of next 2 sts, *ch 4, sk next st and next ch sp, dc in next st, [ch 1, dc in next st] 11 times, ch 4, sk next ch sp and next st**, dc in each of next 5 sts, rep from * around, ending last rep at **, dc in each st across, join with sl st in 3rd ch of beg ch-3.

**Rnd 10:** Ch 3, dc in next st, *ch 4, sk next st and next ch sp, dc in next st, [ch 1, dc in next st] 11 times, ch 4, sk next ch sp and next st**, dc in each of next 3 sts, rep from * around, ending last rep at **, dc in each st across, join with sl st in 3rd ch of beg ch-3.

**Rnd 11:** Ch 1, (sc, ch 3, sc) in first st, ch 3, *({sc, ch 3} twice) in each of next 13 ch sps**, (sc, ch 3, sc) in center st of next dc group, ch 3, rep from * around, ending last rep at **, join with sl st in beg sc. Fasten off.

# Linen Lace

## SKILL LEVEL

INTERMEDIATE

## FINISHED SIZE
14 inches in diameter

## MATERIALS
- DMC Cebellia size 10 crochet cotton (282 yds per ball):
    1 ball #842 coffee cream
- Size 7/1.65mm steel hook or size needed to obtain gauge

## GAUGE
Rnds 1 and 2 = 1½ inches in diameter

## SPECIAL STITCH
**Picot:** Ch 3, sl st in last st made.

## INSTRUCTIONS
### DOILY
**Rnd 1:** Ch 6, sl st in first ch to form ring, ch 4 *(counts as first tr)*, 19 tr in ring, join with sl st in 4th ch of beg ch-4. *(20 tr)*

**Rnd 2:** Ch 6 *(counts as first tr and ch-2 sp)*, [tr in next st, ch 2] around, join with sl st in 4th ch of beg ch-6.

**Rnd 3:** Ch 7 *(counts as first tr and ch-3 sp)* [tr in next st, ch 3] around, join with sl st in 4th ch of beg ch-7.

**Rnd 4:** Ch 8 *(counts as first tr and ch-4 sp)* [tr in next st, ch 4] around, join with sl st in 4th ch of beg ch-8.

**Rnd 5:** Ch 11 *(counts as first tr and ch-7 sp)* [tr in next st, ch 7] around, join with sl st in 4th ch of beg ch-11.

**Rnd 6:** Ch 6, *(tr, ch 2, tr) in next ch sp, ch 2**, tr in next st, ch 2, rep from * around, ending last rep at **, join with sl st in 4th ch of beg ch-6.

**Rnd 7:** Ch 6, *sk next ch sp, (2 tr, ch 2, 2 tr) in next ch sp, ch 2, sk next st**, tr in next st, ch 2, rep from * around, ending last rep at **, join with sl st in 4th ch of beg ch-6.

**Rnd 8:** Ch 6, *sk next ch sp, (3 tr, ch 2, 3 tr) in next ch sp, ch 2, sk next 2 sts**, tr in next st, ch 2, rep from * around, ending last rep at **, join with sl st in 4th ch of beg ch-6.

**Rnd 9:** Ch 1, sc in first st, *ch 5, sk next ch sp, (sc, ch 6, sc) in next ch sp, ch 5, sk next 3 sts**, sc in next st, rep from * around, ending last rep at **, join with sl st in beg sc.

**Rnd 10:** Sl st in each of first 2 chs, ch 1, sc in same ch sp, *ch 3, 9 tr in next ch-6 sp, ch 3, sc in next ch sp, ch 2, sc in next ch sp, ch 4, sc in next ch-6 sp, ch 4, sc in next ch sp, ch 2**, sc in next ch sp, rep from * around, ending last rep at **, join with sl st in beg sc.

**Rnd 11:** Sl st in each ch across to first tr, ch 1, sc in first tr, *[ch 2, sc in next tr] 8 times, ch 5, sk next ch sp, sc in next ch-2 sp, ch 5, sk next st, (sc, ch 5, sc) in next sc, ch 5, sk next ch sp, sc in next ch-2 sp, ch 5**, sc in next tr, rep from * around, ending last rep at **, join with sl st in beg sc.

**Rnd 12:** Ch 1, sc in first ch-2 sp, *[ch 2, sc in next ch-2 sp] 7 times, ch 5, sk next ch sp, sc in next ch sp, ch 3, (sc, ch 5, sc) in next ch sp, ch 3, sc in next ch sp, ch 5, sk next ch sp**, sc in next ch-2 sp, rep from * around, ending last rep at **, join with sl st in beg sc.

**Rnd 13:** Ch 1, sc in first ch-2 sp, *[ch 2, sc in next ch-2 sp] 6 times, ch 5, sk next ch sp, sc in next ch sp, ch 3, (sc, ch 5, sc) in next ch sp, ch 3, sc in next ch sp, ch 5, sk next ch sp**, sc in next ch-2 sp, rep from * around, ending last rep at **, join with sl st in beg sc.

**Rnd 14:** Ch 1, sc in first ch-2 sp, *[ch 2, sc in next ch-2 sp] 5 times, ch 6, sk next ch sp, sc in next ch sp, ch 3, (sc, ch 5, sc) in next ch sp, ch 3, sc in next ch sp, ch 6, sk next ch sp**, sc in next ch-2 sp, rep from * around, ending last rep at **, join with sl st in beg sc.

**Rnd 15:** Ch 1, sc in first ch-2 sp, *[ch 2, sc in next ch-2 sp] 4 times, ch 7, sk next ch sp, sc in next ch sp, ch 3, (sc, ch 5, sc) in next ch sp, ch 3, sc in next ch sp, ch 7, sk next ch sp**, sc in next ch-2 sp, rep from * around, ending last rep at **, join with sl st in beg sc.

**Rnd 16:** Ch 1, sc in first ch-2 sp, *[ch 2, sc in next ch-2 sp] 3 times, ch 8, sk next ch sp, sc in next ch sp, ch 3, (sc, ch 5, sc) in next ch-5 sp, ch 3, sc in next ch sp, ch 8, sk next ch sp**, sc in next ch-2 sp, rep from * around, ending last rep at **, join with sl st in beg sc.

**Rnd 17:** Ch 1, sc in first ch-2 sp, *[ch 2, sc in next ch-2 sp] twice, ch 9, sk next ch sp, sc in next ch sp, ch 3, (sc, ch 5, sc) in next ch sp, ch 3, sc in next ch sp, ch 9, sk next ch sp**, sc in next ch-2 sp, rep from * around, ending last rep at **, join with sl st in beg sc.

**Rnd 18:** Ch 1, sc in first ch-2 sp, *ch 2, sc in next ch-2 sp, ch 10, sk next ch sp, sc in next ch sp, ch 3, (sc, ch 5, sc) in next ch sp, ch 3, sc in next ch sp, ch 10, sk next ch sp**, sc in next ch-2 sp, rep from * around, ending last rep at **, join with sl st in beg sc.

**Rnd 19:** Ch 1, sc in first ch-2 sp, *ch 11, sk next ch sp, sc in next ch sp, ch 3, (sc, ch 5, sc) in next ch sp, ch 3, sc in next ch sp, ch 11, sk next ch sp**, sc in next ch-2 sp, rep from * around, ending last rep at **, join with sl st in beg sc.

**Rnd 20:** Ch 1, sc in first st, *ch 6, (tr, ch 1, tr) in next ch sp, ch 6, sc in next ch sp, ch 3, (sc, ch 5, sc) in next ch sp, ch 3, sc in next ch sp, ch 6, (tr, ch 1, tr) in next ch sp, ch 6**, sc in next st, rep from * around, ending last rep at **, join with sl st in beg sc.

**Rnd 21:** Sl st in each of first 2 chs, ch 1, sc in same ch sp, *ch 4, tr in next ch sp, (ch 1, tr) 3 times in same ch sp, ch 6, sk next ch sp, sc in next ch sp, ch 3, sc in next ch sp, ch 3, (tr, ch 1) twice in same ch sp, tr in same ch sp, ch 3, sc in same ch sp, ch 3, sc in next ch sp, ch 6, sk next ch sp, tr in next ch sp, (ch 1, tr) 3 times in same ch sp, ch 4, sc in next ch sp, ch 2**, sc in next ch sp, rep from * around, ending last rep at **, join with sl st in beg sc.

**Rnd 22:** Sl st across to first ch-1 sp, ch 5, tr in same ch sp, *({ch 1, tr} twice) in each of next 2 ch sps, ch 6, sk next ch sp, sc in next ch-3 sp, ch 6, ({tr, ch 1} twice) in each of next 2 ch sps, (tr, ch 1, tr) in next ch sp, ch 6, sk next ch sp, sc in next ch-3 sp, ch 6, sk next ch sp, (tr, ch 1, tr) in next ch sp, ({ch 1, tr} twice) in each of next 2 ch sps, ch 6, sk next ch sp, sc in next ch-2 sp, ch 6, sk next ch sp**, (tr, ch 1, tr) in next ch sp, rep from * around, ending last rep at **, join with sl st in 4th ch of beg ch-5.

**Rnd 23:** Ch 1, (sc, **picot**—*see Special Stitch,* sc) in first ch sp, *[sc in next ch sp, (sc, picot, sc) in next ch sp] twice, (2 sc, picot, 2 sc) in each of next 2 ch sps, [(sc, picot, sc) in next ch sp, sc in next ch sp] twice, (sc, picot, sc) in next ch sp, (2 sc, picot, 2 sc) in each of next 2 ch sps**, (sc, picot, sc) in next ch sp, rep from * around, ending last rep at **, join with sl st in beg sc. Fasten off.

# Tempest

## SKILL LEVEL

INTERMEDIATE

## FINISHED SIZE
12 inches in diameter

## MATERIALS
- Aunt Lydia's Classic size 10 crochet cotton (350 yds per ball): 1 ball #480 delft
- Size 7/1.65mm steel crochet hook or size needed to obtain gauge

## GAUGE

Rnd 1 = 1 inch in diameter

## SPECIAL STITCHES
**Cluster (cl):** Holding last lp of each st on hook, 3 tr in next ch sp, yo, pull through all lps on hook.
**Shell:** (2 tr, ch 2, 2 tr) in next ch sp.
**Picot:** Ch 3, sl st in 3rd ch from hook.

## INSTRUCTIONS
### DOILY
**Rnd 1:** Ch 6, sl st in first ch to form ring, ch 4 *(counts as first tr)* 23 tr in ring, join with sl st in 4th ch of beg ch-4. *(24 tr)*

**Rnd 2:** Ch 1, sc in first st, ch 4, sk next st, [sc in next st, ch 4, sk next st] around, join with sl st in beg sc.

**Rnd 3:** Sl st in each of first 2 chs, ch 1, sc in same ch sp, ch 4, [sc in next ch sp, ch 4] around, join with sl st in beg sc.

**Rnd 4:** Sl st in each of first 2 chs, ch 1, sc in same ch sp, ch 5, [sc in next ch sp, ch 5] around, join with sl st in beg sc.

**Rnd 5:** Sl st in each of first 2 chs, ch 1, sc in same ch sp, ch 6, [sc in next ch sp, ch 6] around, join with sl st in beg sc.

**Rnd 6:** Sl st in each of first 3 chs, ch 1, sc in same ch sp, *ch 7, **cl** *(see Special Stitches)* in next ch sp, ch 7**, sc in next ch sp, rep from * around, ending last rep at **, join with sl st in beg sc.

**Rnd 7:** Sl st in each of first 3 chs, ch 1, sc in same ch sp, *ch 5, cl in same ch sp, ch 3, cl in next ch sp, ch 5, sc in same ch sp, ch 3**, sc in next ch sp, rep from * around, ending last rep at **, join with sl st in beg sc.

**Rnd 8:** Sl st in each of first 2 chs, ch 1, sc in same ch sp, *ch 5, cl in same ch sp, ch 3, cl in next ch sp, ch 3, (cl, ch 5, sc) in next ch sp, ch 3, (tr, ch 1, tr) in next ch sp, ch 3**, sc in next ch sp, rep from * around, ending last rep at **, join with sl st in beg sc.

**Rnd 9:** Sl st in each of first 2 chs, ch 1, sc in same ch sp, *ch 5, sc in next ch sp, ch 7, sc in next ch sp, ch 5, sc in next ch sp, ch 5, **shell** *(see Special Stitches)*, ch 5**, sc in next ch sp, rep from * around, ending last rep at **, join with sl st in beg sc.

**Rnd 10:** Sl st in each of first 2 chs, ch 1, sc in same ch sp, *ch 3, 9 tr in next ch-7 sp, ch 3, sc in next ch sp, ch 4, sc in next ch sp, ch 3, shell, ch 3, sc in next ch sp, ch 4**, sc in next ch sp, rep from * around, ending last rep at **, join with sl st in beg sc.

**Rnd 11:** Sl st in first ch sp, ch 1, sc in same ch sp, *ch 4, tr in next tr, [ch 1, tr in next tr] 8 times, ch 3, sc in next ch sp, ch 4, sc in next ch sp, ch 5, sk next ch sp, (3 tr, ch 2, 3 tr) in ch sp of next shell, ch 5, sk next ch sp, sc in next ch sp, ch 4**, sc in next ch sp, rep from * around, ending last rep at **, join with sl st in beg sc.

**Rnd 12:** Sl st across to first ch-1 sp, ch 1, sc in same ch-1 sp, *[ch 2, sc in next ch-1 sp] 7 times, ch 4, sk next ch sp, sc in next ch sp, ch 5, sk next ch sp, (shell, ch 2, 2 tr) in next ch sp, ch 5, sk next ch sp, sc in next ch sp, ch 4, sk next ch sp**, sc in next ch-1 sp, rep from * around, ending last rep at **, join with sl st in beg sc.

**Rnd 13:** Ch 1, sc in first ch-2 sp, *[ch 2, sc in next ch-2 sp] 6 times, [ch 4, sc in next ch sp] twice, ch 4, shell, ch 2, shell, [ch 4, sc in next ch sp] twice, ch 4**, sc in next ch-2 sp, rep from * around, ending last rep at **, join with sl st in beg sc.

**Rnd 14:** Ch 1, sc in first ch-2 sp, *[ch 2, sc in next ch-2 sp] 5 times, ch 3, sk next ch sp, (tr, ch 2, tr) in next ch sp, ch 3, sk next ch sp, shell, ch 2, 2 tr in next ch sp, ch 2, shell, ch 3, sk next ch sp, (tr, ch 2, tr) in next ch sp, ch 3, sk next ch sp**, sc in next ch-2 sp, rep from * around, ending last rep at **, join with sl st in beg sc.

**Rnd 15:** Ch 1, sc in first ch-2 sp, *[ch 2, sc in next ch-2 sp] 4 times, ch 5, sk next ch sp, (tr, ch 2, tr) in next ch sp, ch 5, sk next ch sp, shell, [ch 2, 2 tr in next ch sp] twice, ch 2, shell, ch 5, sk next ch sp, (tr, ch 2, tr) in next ch sp, ch 5, sk next ch sp**, sc in next ch-2 sp, rep from * around, ending last rep at **, join with sl st in beg sc.

**Rnd 16:** Ch 1, sc in first ch-2 sp, *[ch 2, sc in next ch-2 sp] 3 times, ch 5, sk next ch sp, (tr, ch 2, tr) in next ch sp, ch 5, sk next ch sp, shell, [ch 2, 2 tr in next ch sp] 3 times, ch 2, shell, ch 5, sk next ch sp, (tr, ch 2, tr) in next ch sp, ch 5, sk next ch sp**, sc in next ch-2 sp, rep from * around, ending last rep at **, join with sl st in beg sc.

**Rnd 17:** Ch 1, sc in first ch-2 sp, *[ch 2, sc in next ch-2 sp] twice, ch 5, sk next ch sp, (tr, ch 2, tr) in next ch sp, ch 5, sk next ch sp, shell, [ch 2, 2 tr in next ch sp] 4 times, ch 2, shell, ch 5, sk next ch sp, (tr, ch 2, tr) in next ch sp, ch 5, sk next ch sp**, sc in next ch-2 sp, rep from * around, ending last rep at **, join with sl st in beg sc.

**Rnd 18:** Ch 1, sc in first ch-2 sp, *ch 2, sc in next ch-2 sp, ch 5, sk next ch sp, (tr, ch 2, tr) in next ch sp, ch 5, sk next ch sp, shell, [ch 2, 2 tr in next ch sp] 5 times, ch 2, shell, ch 5, sk next ch sp, (tr, ch 2, tr) in next ch sp, ch 5, sk next ch sp**, sc in next ch-2 sp, rep from * around, ending last rep at **, join with sl st in beg sc.

**Rnd 19:** Ch 1, sc in first ch-2 sp, *ch 5, sk next ch sp, (tr, ch 2, tr) in next ch sp, ch 6, sk next ch sp, shell, [ch 2, 2 tr in next ch sp] 6 times, ch 2, shell, ch 6, sk next ch sp, (tr, ch 2, tr) in next ch sp, ch 5, sk next ch sp**, sc in next ch-2 sp, rep from * around, ending last rep at **, join with sl st in beg sc.

**Rnd 20:** Ch 1, sc in each tr around with (3 sc, **picot**—*see Special Stitches,* 3 sc) in each ch-2 sp, join with sl st in beg sc. Fasten off.

# Peach Parfait

## SKILL LEVEL
INTERMEDIATE

## FINISHED SIZE
11½ inches in diameter

## MATERIALS
- Aunt Lydia's size 10 crochet cotton (350 yds per ball):
  1 ball #424 light peach

- Size 7/1.65mm steel crochet hook or size needed to obtain gauge

## GAUGE
Rnd 1 = ¾ inch in diameter

## SPECIAL STITCH
**Cluster (cl):** Holding last lp of each st on hook, 3 dc in next ch sp, yo, pull through all lps on hook.

## INSTRUCTIONS

### DOILY
**Rnd 1:** Ch 6, sl st in first ch to form ring, ch 3 *(counts as first dc)*, 17 dc in ring, join with sl st in 3rd ch of beg ch-3. *(18 dc)*

**Rnd 2:** Ch 3, dc in same st, ch 5, sk next 2 sts, [2 dc in next st, ch 5, sk next 2 sts] around, join with sl st in 3rd ch of beg ch-3.

**Rnd 3:** Ch 3, dc in next st, *ch 3, sc in next ch sp, ch 3**, dc in each of next 2 sts, rep from * around, ending last rep at **, join with sl st in 3rd ch of beg ch-3.

**Rnd 4:** Ch 3, dc in next st, *[ch 3, sc in next ch sp] twice, ch 3**, dc in each of next 2 sts, rep from * around, ending last rep at **, join with sl st in 3rd ch of beg ch-3.

**Rnd 5:** Ch 3, dc in next st, *ch 4, sk next ch sp, (sc, ch 6, sc) in next ch sp, ch 4**, dc in each of next 2 st, rep from * around, ending last rep at **, join with sl st in 3rd ch of beg ch-3.

**Rnd 6:** Ch 3, dc in next st, *ch 2, sc in next ch sp, ch 2, 7 dc in next ch-6 sp, ch 2, sc in next ch sp, ch 2**, dc in each of next 2 sts, rep from * around, ending last rep at **, join with sl st in 3rd ch of beg ch-3.

**Rnd 7:** Ch 3, dc in next st, *ch 2, sc in next ch sp, ch 2, [sc in next st, ch 2] 7 times, sc in next ch sp, ch 2**, dc in each of next 2 sts, rep from * around, ending last rep at **, join with sl st in 3rd ch of beg ch-3.

**Rnd 8:** Ch 3, dc in next st, *ch 2, sc in next ch sp, ch 3, sk next ch sp, [sc in next ch sp, ch 2] 5 times, sc in next ch sp, ch 3, sk next ch sp, sc in next ch sp, ch 2\*\*, dc in each of next 2 sts, rep from \* around, ending last rep at \*\*, join with sl st in 3rd ch of beg ch-3.

**Rnd 9:** Ch 3, dc in next st, \*ch 2, sc in next ch sp, ch 4, sk next ch sp, sc in next ch sp, [ch 2, sc in next ch sp] 4 times, ch 4, sk next ch sp, sc in next ch sp, ch 2\*\*, dc in each of next 2 sts, rep from \* around, ending last rep at \*\*, join with sl st in 3rd ch of beg ch-3.

**Rnd 10:** Ch 3, dc in next st, \*ch 2, sc in next ch sp, ch 5, sk next ch sp, sc in next ch sp, [ch 2, sc in next ch sp] 3 times, ch 5, sk next ch sp, sc in next ch sp, ch 2\*\*, dc in each of next 2 sts, rep from \* around, ending last rep at \*\*, join with sl st in 3rd ch of beg ch-3.

**Rnd 11:** Ch 3, dc in next st, \*ch 2, sc in next ch sp, ch 6, sk next ch sp, sc in next ch sp, [ch 2, sc in next ch sp] twice, ch 6, sk next ch sp, sc in next ch sp, ch 2\*\*, dc in each of next 2 sts, rep from \* around, ending last rep at \*\*, join with sl st in 3rd ch of beg ch-3.

**Rnd 12:** Ch 3, dc in next st, \*ch 2, sc in next ch sp, ch 8, sk next ch sp, sc in next ch sp, ch 2, sc in next ch sp, ch 8, sk next ch sp, sc in next ch sp, ch 2\*\*, dc in each of next 2 sts, rep from \* around, ending last rep at \*\*, join with sl st in 3rd ch of beg ch-3.

**Rnd 13:** Ch 3, dc in next st, \*ch 4, sc in next ch sp, ch 5, **cl** *(see Special Stitch)* in next ch sp, ch 5, sc in next ch-2 sp, ch 5, cl in next ch sp, ch 5, sc in next ch sp, ch 4\*\*, dc in each of next 2 sts, rep from \* around, ending last rep at \*\*, join with sl st in 3rd ch of beg ch-3.

**Rnd 14:** Ch 3, dc in next st, \*ch 4, sc in next ch sp, ch 4, cl in next ch sp, ch 4, sc in next ch sp, ch 6, sc in next ch sp, ch 4, cl in next ch sp, ch 4, sc in next ch sp, ch 4\*\*, dc in each of next 2 sts, rep from \* around, ending last rep at \*\*, join with sl st in 3rd ch of beg ch-3.

**Rnd 15:** Ch 3, dc in same st, \*ch 2, 2 dc in next st, ch 4, sc in next ch sp, ch 4, cl in next ch sp, ch 4, sc in next ch sp, ch 3, 7 dc in next ch-6 sp, ch 3, sc in next ch sp, ch 4, cl in next ch sp, ch 4, sc in next ch sp, ch 4\*\*, 2 dc in next st, rep from \* around, ending last rep at \*\*, join with sl st in 3rd ch of beg ch-3.

**Rnd 16:** Ch 3, dc in next st, \*ch 3, dc in each of next 2 sts, ch 4, sc in next ch sp, ch 4, cl in next ch sp, ch 4, sc in next ch sp, ch 3, sc in next st, [ch 2, sc in next st] 6 times, ch 3, sc in next ch sp, ch 4, cl in next ch sp, ch 4, sc in next ch sp, ch 4\*\*, dc in each of next 2 sts, rep from * around, ending last rep at **, join with sl st in 3rd ch of beg ch-3.

**Rnd 17:** Ch 3, *2 dc in next st, ch 3, 2 dc in next st, dc in next st, ch 4, sc in next ch sp, ch 4, cl in next ch sp, ch 4, sc in next ch sp, ch 4, sk next ch sp, sc in next ch sp, [ch 2, sc in next ch sp] 5 times, ch 4, sk next ch sp, sc in next ch sp, ch 4, cl in next ch sp, ch 4, sc in next ch sp, ch 4**, dc in next st, rep from * around, ending last rep at **, join with sl st in 3rd ch of beg ch-3.

**Rnd 18:** Ch 3, *dc in next st, 2 dc in next st, ch 3, 2 dc in next st, dc in each of next 2 sts, ch 4, sc in next ch sp, ch 4, cl in next ch sp, ch 4, sc in next ch sp, ch 5, sk next ch sp, sc in next ch sp, [ch 2, sc in next ch sp] 4 times, ch 5, sk next ch sp, sc in next ch sp, ch 4, cl in next ch sp, ch 4, sc in next ch sp, ch 4**, dc in next st, rep from * around, ending last rep at **, join with sl st in 3rd ch of beg ch-3.

**Rnd 19:** Ch 3, *dc in each of next 2 sts, 2 dc in next st, ch 3, 2 dc in next st, dc in each of next 3 sts, ch 4, sc in next ch sp, ch 4, cl in next ch sp, ch 4, sc in next ch sp, ch 6, sk next ch sp, sc in next ch sp, [ch 2, sc in next ch sp] 3 times, ch 6, sk next ch sp, sc in next ch sp, ch 4, cl in next ch sp, ch 4, sc in next ch sp, ch 4**, dc in next st, rep from * around, ending last rep at **, join with sl st in 3rd ch of beg ch-3.

**Rnd 20:** Ch 3, *dc in each of next 3 sts, 2 dc in next st, ch 4, 2 dc in next st, dc in each of next 4 sts, ch 4, sc in next ch sp, ch 4, cl in next ch sp, ch 4, sc in next ch sp, ch 7, sk next ch sp, sc in next ch sp, [ch 2, sc in next ch sp] twice, ch 7, sk next ch sp, sc in next ch sp, ch 4, cl in next ch sp, ch 4, sc in next ch sp, ch 4**, dc in next st, rep from * around, ending last rep at **, join with sl st in 3rd ch of beg ch-3.

**Rnd 21:** Ch 3, *dc in each of next 4 sts, 2 dc in next st, ch 4, 2 dc in next st, dc in each of next 5 sts, ch 4, sc in next ch sp, ch 4, cl in next ch sp, ch 4, sc in next ch sp, ch 8, sk next ch sp, sc in next ch sp, ch 2, sc in next ch sp, ch 8, sk next ch sp, sc in next ch sp, ch 4, cl in next ch sp, ch 4, sc in next ch sp, ch 4**, dc in next st, rep from * around, ending last rep at **, join with sl st in 3rd ch of beg ch-3.

**Rnd 22:** Ch 3, *dc in each of next 5 sts, 2 dc in next st, ch 6, 2 dc in next st, dc in each of next 6 sts, ch 4, sc in next ch sp, ch 4, cl in next ch sp, ch 4, sc in next ch sp, ch 9, sk next ch sp, sc in next ch sp, ch 9, sk next ch sp, sc in next ch sp, ch 4, cl in next ch sp, ch 4, sc in next ch sp, ch 4**, dc in next st, rep from * around, ending last rep at **, join with sl st in 3rd ch of beg ch-3.

**Rnd 23:** Ch 3, *dc in each of next 7 sts, ch 3, sc in next ch sp, ch 3, dc in each of next 8 sts, ch 4, sc in next ch sp, ch 4, cl in next ch sp, ch 4, sc in next ch sp, ch 5, sc in next ch-9 sp, ch 6, sc in next ch-9 sp, ch 5, sc in next ch sp, ch 4, cl in next ch sp, ch 4, sc in next ch sp, ch 4**, dc in next st, rep from * around, ending last rep at **, join with sl st in 3rd ch of beg ch-3.

**Rnd 24:** Ch 2 *(does not count as st)*, **dc dec** *(see Stitch Guide)* in next 7 sts, *ch 5, sc in next ch sp, ch 3, sc in next ch sp, ch 5, dc dec in next 8 sts, ch 5, (sc, ch 4, sc) in next ch sp, ch 4, sc in next ch sp, ch 4, sc in next cl, ch 4, sc in next ch sp, ch 4, ({sc, ch 4} twice) in each of next 3 ch sps, sc in next ch sp, ch 4, sc in next cl, ch 4, sc in next ch sp, ch 4, (sc, ch 4, sc) in next ch sp, ch 5**, dc dec in next 8 sts, rep from * around, ending last rep at **, join with sl st in beg dc dec.

**Rnd 25:** [Ch 5, sl st in 3rd ch from hook, ch 2, sc in next ch sp] around, ending with ch 5, sl st in 3rd ch from hook, ch 2, join with sl st in base of beg ch-5. Fasten off.

# Autumn Acorns

## SKILL LEVEL

INTERMEDIATE

## FINISHED SIZE
10 inches in diameter

## MATERIALS
- Aunt Lydia's Classic size 10 crochet cotton (1000 yds per ball):
  1 ball #226 natural
- Size 6/1.80mm steel hook or size needed to obtain gauge

## GAUGE
Rnd 1 = 1 inches in diameter

## INSTRUCTIONS

### DOILY

**Rnd 1:** Ch 6, sl st in first ch to form ring, ch 4 *(counts as first tr)*, tr in ring, ch 2, [2 tr in ring, ch 2] 7 times, join with sl st in 4th ch of beg ch-4.

**Rnd 2:** Ch 4, tr in next st, ch 3, [tr in each of next 2 sts, ch 3] around, join with sl st in 4th ch of beg ch-4.

**Rnd 3:** Ch 4, tr in next st, *ch 3, (tr, ch 2, tr) in next ch sp, ch 3**, tr in each of next 2 sts, rep from * around, ending last rep at **, join with sl st in 4th ch of beg ch-4.

**Rnd 4:** Ch 4, tr in next st, *ch 3, sk next ch sp, (tr, ch 2, tr) in next ch sp, ch 3, sk next ch sp**, tr in each of next 2 sts, rep from * around, ending last rep at **, join with sl st in 4th ch of beg ch-4.

**Rnd 5:** Ch 4, tr in next st, *ch 3, sk next ch sp, (2 tr, ch 2, 2 tr) in next ch sp, ch 3, sk next ch sp**, tr in each of next 2 sts, rep from * around, ending last rep at **, join with sl st in 4th ch of beg ch-4.

**Rnd 6:** Ch 4, tr in next st, *ch 5, sk next ch sp, (3 tr, ch 2, 3 tr) in next ch sp, ch 5, sk next ch sp**, tr in each of next 2 sts, rep from * around, ending last rep at **, join with sl st in 4th ch of beg ch-4.

**Rnd 7:** Ch 4, tr in next st, *ch 4, sc in next ch sp, ch 4, ({2 tr, ch 2} twice, 2 tr) in next ch sp, ch 4, sc in next ch sp, ch 4**, tr in each of next 2 sts, rep from * around, ending last rep at **, join with sl st in 4th ch of beg ch-4.

**Rnd 8:** Ch 4, tr in next st, *[ch 4, sc in next ch sp] twice, ch 4, (2 tr, ch 2, 2 tr) in next ch sp, ch 2, (2 tr, ch 2, 2 tr) in next ch sp, ch 4, [sc in next ch sp, ch 4] twice**, tr in each of next 2 sts, rep from * around, ending last rep at **, join with sl st in 4th ch of beg ch-4.

**Rnd 9:** Ch 1, sc in first st, *ch 6, sc in next ch sp, ch 4, sk next ch sp, sc in next ch sp, ch 4, (3 tr, ch 2, 3 tr) in next ch sp, ch 2, sk next ch sp, (3 tr, ch 2, 3 tr) in next ch sp, ch 4, sc in next ch sp, ch 4, sk next ch sp**, sc in next ch sp, rep from * around, ending last rep at **, ch 4, sc in next ch sp, ch 4, join with sl st in beg sc.

**Rnd 10:** Sl st in first ch sp, ch 4, 8 tr in same ch sp, *ch 4, sk next ch sp, sc in next ch sp, ch 4, (3 tr, ch 2, 3 tr) in next ch sp, ch 3, sk next ch sp, (3 tr, ch 2, 3 tr) in next ch sp, ch 4, sc in next ch sp, ch

4, sk next ch sp**, 9 tr in next ch sp, rep from * around, ending last rep at **, join with sl st in 4th ch of beg ch-4.

**Rnd 11:** Ch 1, sc in first st, [ch 2, sc in next st] 8 times, *ch 4, sk next ch sp, sc in next ch sp, ch 4, (3 tr, ch 2, 3 tr) in next ch sp, ch 2, (tr, ch 1, tr) in next ch sp, ch 2, (3 tr, ch 2, 3 tr) in next ch sp, ch 4, sc in next ch sp, ch 4, sk next ch sp**, sc in next st, rep from * around, ending last rep at **, join with sl st in beg sc.

**Rnd 12:** Sl st in first ch sp, ch 3, **tr dec** *(see Stitch Guide)* in next 7 ch sps, *ch 6, sk next ch sp, sc in next ch sp, ch 4, ({2 tr, ch 2} twice, 2 tr) in next ch sp, ch 4, sk next ch sp, sc in next ch sp, ch 4, sk next ch sp, ({2 tr, ch 2} twice, 2 tr) in next ch sp, ch 4, sc in next ch sp, ch 6, sk next ch sp**, tr dec in next 8 ch sps, rep from * around, ending last rep at **, join with sl st in top of first tr dec.

**Rnd 13:** Sl st in first ch sp, ch 1, ({sc, ch 3} 3 times, sc) in same ch sp, *[ch 3, (sc, ch 3, sc) in next ch sp] 8 times, ch 3, ({sc, ch 3} 3 times, sc) in next ch sp**, ch 3, ({sc, ch 3} 3 times, sc) in next ch sp, rep from * around, ending last rep at **, ch 3, ({sc, ch 3} 3 times, sc) in next ch sp, rep from * around, ending last rep at **, join with sl st in beg sc. Fasten off.

# Silver Cones

## SKILL LEVEL

INTERMEDIATE

## FINISHED SIZE
8 inches in diameter

## MATERIALS
- Size 10 crochet cotton:
    150 yds silver
- Size 7/1.65mm steel hook or size needed to obtain gauge

## GAUGE
Rnd 1 = 1 inch in diameter

## SPECIAL STITCH

**Cluster (cl):** Holding last lp on hook, 3 tr in next ch sp, yo, pull through all lps on hook.

## INSTRUCTIONS

### DOILY

**Rnd 1:** Ch 6, sl st in first ch to form ring, ch 4 *(counts as first tr)*, 23 tr in ring, join with sl st in 4th ch of beg ch-4. *(24 tr)*

**Rnd 2:** Ch 1, sc in first st, ch 4, sk next 2 sts, [sc in next st, ch 4, sk next 2 sts] around, join with sl st in beg sc.

**Rnd 3:** Sl st in first ch sp, ch 4, (tr, ch 3, sc, ch 3, 2 tr) in same ch sp, *ch 4, sc in next ch sp, ch 4**, (2 tr, ch 3, sc, ch 3, 2 tr) in next ch sp, rep from * around, ending last rep at **, join with sl st in 4th ch of beg ch-4.

**Rnd 4:** Ch 4, tr in next st, tr in next ch sp, *ch 2, tr in next ch sp, tr in each of next 2 sts, ch 5, sc in next ch sp, ch 3, sc in next ch sp, ch 5**, tr in each of next 2 sts, tr in next ch sp, rep from * around, ending last rep at **, join with sl st in 4th ch of beg ch-4.

**Rnd 5:** Ch 4, tr in each of next 2 sts, *ch 3, sc in next ch sp, ch 3, tr in each of next 3 sts, ch 4, sc in next ch sp, ch 3, **cl** *(see Special Stitches)* in next ch sp, ch 3, sc in next ch sp, ch 4**, tr in each of next 3 sts, rep from * around, ending last rep at **, join with sl st in 4th ch of beg ch-4.

**Rnd 6:** Ch 4, tr in each of next 2 sts, *ch 4, sk next 2 ch sps, tr in each of next 3 sts, ch 4, sc in next ch sp, ch 3, [cl in next ch sp, ch 3] twice, sc in next ch sp, ch 4**, tr in each of next 3 sts, rep from * around, ending last rep at **, join with sl st in 4th ch of beg ch 4.

**Rnd 7:** Ch 4, tr in each of next 2 sts, *ch 4, sc in next ch sp, ch 4, tr in each of next 3 sts, ch 4, sc in next ch sp, [ch 3, cl in next ch sp] 3 times, ch 3, sc in next ch sp, ch 4**, tr in each of next 3 sts, rep from * around, ending last rep at **, join with sl st in 4th ch of beg ch-4.

**Rnd 8:** Ch 1, sc in next tr, *ch 9, sk next 2 ch sps and next tr, sc in next tr, ch 5, sk next ch sp, [cl in next ch sp, ch 3] 3 times, cl in next ch sp, ch 5, sk next ch sp and next tr**, sc in next tr, rep from * around, ending last rep at **, join with sl st in beg sc.

**Rnd 9:** Ch 1, sc in first st, ch 3, (2 tr, ch 1, 2 tr) in next ch sp, *ch 3, sc in next sc, ch 3, (2 tr, ch 1, 2 tr) in next ch sp, ch 3, sc in same ch sp, ch 3, [cl in next ch sp, ch 2] twice, cl in next ch sp, ch 3, sc in next ch sp, ch 3, (2 tr, ch 1, 2 tr) in same ch sp, ch 3**, sc in next sc, ch 3, (2 tr, ch 1, 2 tr) in next ch sp, rep from * around, ending with last rep at **, join with sl st in beg sc.

**Rnd 10:** Sl st in first ch sp, ch 1, sc in same ch sp, *ch 3, (2 tr, ch 1, 2 tr) in next ch sp, [ch 3, sc in next ch sp] twice, ch 3, (2 tr, ch 1, 2 tr) in next ch sp, ch 3, [sc in next ch sp, ch 3] twice, cl in next ch sp, ch 2, cl in next ch sp, ch 3, [sc in next ch sp, ch 3] twice, (2 tr, ch 1, 2 tr) in next ch sp**, [ch 3, sc in next sc] twice, rep from * around, ending last rep at **, ch 3, sc in next ch sp, ch 3, join with sl st in beg sc.

**Rnd 11:** Sl st in first ch sp, ch 1, sc in same ch sp, ch 4, [sc in next ch sp, ch 4] 8 times, *cl in next ch sp, ch 4**, [sc in next ch sp, ch 4] 15 times, rep from * around, ending last rep at **, [sc in next ch sp, ch 4] around, join with sl st in beg sc.

**Rnds 12 & 13:** Sl st in first ch sp, ch 1, sc in same ch sp, ch 4, [sc in next ch sp, ch 4] around, join with sl st in beg sc.

**Rnd 14:** Sl st in first ch sp, ch 1, ({sc, ch 3} twice) in same ch sp and in each ch sp around, join with sl st in beg sc. Fasten off.

# Fanfare

## SKILL LEVEL

INTERMEDIATE

## FINISHED SIZE
13 inches in diameter

## MATERIALS
- DMC Cebelia size 10 crochet cotton (282 yds per ball):
  1 ball ecru
- Size 6/1.80mm steel hook or size needed to obtain gauge

## GAUGE
Rnd 1 = 1 inch in diameter

## INSTRUCTIONS

### DOILY

**Rnd 1:** Ch 8, sl st in first ch to form ring, ch 3 *(counts as first dc)*, 23 dc in ring, join with sl st in 3rd ch of beg ch-3. *(24 dc)*

**Rnd 2:** Ch 4, 2 tr in same st, *ch 5, sk next st, sc in next st, ch 5, sk next st**, 3 tr in next st, rep from * around, ending last rep at **, join with sl st in 4th ch of beg ch-4.

**Rnd 3:** Ch 4, tr in each of next 2 sts, *ch 5, sc in next ch sp, ch 3, sc in next ch sp, ch 5**, tr in each of next 3 sts, rep from * around, ending last rep at **, join with sl st in 4th ch of beg ch-4.

**Rnd 4:** Ch 6 *(counts as first tr and ch-2 sp)*, *sk next st, tr in next st, ch 6, sc in next ch sp, ch 3, (tr, ch 2, tr) in next ch sp, ch 3, sc in next ch sp, ch 6**, tr in next st, ch 2, rep from * around, ending last rep at **, join with sl st in 4th ch of beg ch-6.

**Rnd 5:** Ch 1, (sc, ch 5, sc) in first ch sp, *ch 3, sc in next ch sp, ch 3, sk next ch sp, (2 tr, ch 3, 2 tr) in next ch sp, ch 3, sk next ch sp, sc in next ch sp, ch 3**, (sc, ch 5, sc) in next ch sp, rep from * around, ending last rep at **, join with sl st in beg sc.

**Rnd 6:** Sl st in next ch sp, ch 4, 8 tr in same ch sp, *ch 3, sc in next ch sp, ch 5, sk next ch sp, (3 tr, ch 3, 3 tr) in next ch sp, ch 5, sk next ch sp, sc in next ch sp, ch 3**, 9 tr in next ch sp, rep from * around, ending last rep at **, join with sl st in 4th ch of beg ch-4.

**Rnd 7:** Ch 5 *(counts as first tr and ch-1 sp)*, tr in next st, [ch 1, tr in next st] 7 times, *ch 5, sk next ch sp, sc in next ch sp, ch 5, ({2 tr, ch 2} twice, 2 tr) in next ch sp, ch 5, sc in next ch sp, ch 5, sk next ch sp**, tr in next tr, [ch 1, tr in next st] 8 times, rep from * around, ending last rep at **, join with sl st in 4th ch of beg ch-5.

**Rnd 8:** Ch 1, sc in first ch sp, *[ch 2, sc in next ch sp] 7 times, ch 4, sc in next ch sp, ch 3, sc in next ch sp, ch 4, 3 tr in next ch-2 sp, ch 3, 3 tr in next ch-2 sp, ch 4, sc in next ch sp, ch 3, sc in next ch sp, ch 4**, sc in next ch-1 sp, rep from * around, ending last rep at **, join with sl st in beg sc.

**Rnd 9:** Ch 1, sc in first ch-2 sp, *[ch 2, sc in next ch-2 sp] 6 times, ch 4, sk next ch sp, sc in next ch sp, ch 5, sk next ch sp, ({2 tr, ch 2} twice, 2 tr) in next ch sp, ch 5, sk next ch sp, sc in next ch sp, ch 4, sk next ch sp**, sc in next ch-2 sp, rep from * around, ending last rep at **, join with sl st in beg sc.

**Rnd 10:** Ch 1, sc in first ch-2 sp, *[ch 2, sc in next ch-2 sp] 5 times, ch 4, sk next ch sp, sc in next ch sp, ch 5, (3 tr, ch 2, 3 tr) in next ch sp, ch 2, (3 tr, ch 2, 3 tr) in next ch sp, ch 5, sc in next ch sp, ch 4, sk next ch sp**, sc in next ch-2 sp, rep from * around, ending last rep at **, join with sl st in beg sc.

**Rnd 11:** Ch 1, sc in first ch-2 sp, *[ch 2, sc in next ch-2 sp] 4 times, ch 5, sk next ch sp, sc in next ch sp, ch 5, (2 tr, ch 2, 2 tr) in next ch sp, ch 2, 2 tr in next ch sp, ch 2, (2 tr, ch 2, 2 tr) in next ch sp, ch 5, sc in next ch sp, ch 5, sk next ch sp**, sc in next ch-2 sp, rep from * around, ending last rep at **, join with sl st in beg sc.

**Rnd 12:** Ch 1, sc in first ch-2 sp, *[ch 2, sc in next ch-2 sp] 3 times, ch 5, sk next ch sp, sc in next ch sp, ch 5, (3 tr, ch 2, 3 tr) in next ch sp, ch 2, [3 tr in next ch sp, ch 2] twice, (3 tr, ch 2, 3 tr) in next ch sp, ch 5, sc in next ch sp, ch 5, sk next ch sp**, sc in next ch-2 sp, rep from * around, ending last rep at **, join with sl st in beg sc.

**Rnd 13:** Ch 1, sc in first ch-2 sp, *[ch 2, sc in next ch-2 sp] twice, ch 7, sk next ch sp, sc in next ch sp, ch 5, [(2 tr, ch 2, 2 tr) in next ch sp, ch 2] 4 times, (2 tr, ch 2, 2 tr) in next ch sp, ch 5, sc in next ch sp, ch 4, sk next ch sp**, sc in next ch-2 sp, rep from * around, ending last rep at **, join with sl st in beg sc.

**Rnd 14:** Ch 1, sc in first ch-2 sp, *ch 2, sc in next ch-2 sp, ch 8, sk next ch sp, sc in next ch sp, ch 5, (3 tr, ch 2, 3 tr) in next ch sp, [ch 2, (3 tr, ch 2, 3 tr) in next ch sp] 4 times, ch 5, sc in next ch sp, ch 8, sk next ch sp**, sc in next ch-2 sp, rep from * around, ending last rep at **, join with sl st in beg sc.

**Rnd 15:** Ch 1, sc in first ch-2 sp, *ch 9, sk next ch sp, sc in next ch sp, ch 5, (2 tr, ch 2, 2 tr) in next ch sp, [ch 4, sc in next ch sp, ch 4, (2 tr, ch 2, 2 tr) in next ch sp] 4 times, ch 5, sc in next ch sp, ch 9, sk next ch sp**, sc in next ch-2 sp, rep from * around, ending last rep at **, join with sl st in beg sc.

**Rnd 16:** Ch 1, sc in first st, *ch 10, sk next ch sp, sc in next ch sp, ch 5, (3 tr, ch 2, 3 tr) in next ch sp, [ch 4, sc in next ch sp, ch 2, sc in next ch sp, ch 4, (3 tr, ch 2, 3 tr) in next ch sp] 4 times, ch 5, sc in next ch sp, ch 10, sk next ch sp**, sc in next st, rep from * around, ending last rep at **, join with sl st in beg sc. Fasten off.

# Regency

## SKILL LEVEL

INTERMEDIATE

## FINISHED SIZE
11 inches in diameter

## MATERIALS
- Aunt Lydia's Classic size 10 crochet cotton (400 yds per ball):
  1 ball #419 ecru
- Size 6/1.80mm steel crochet hook or size needed to obtain gauge

## GAUGE

Rnds 1 and 2 = 1¾ inches in diameter

## INSTRUCTIONS

### DOILY

**Rnd 1:** Ch 6, sl st in first ch to form ring, ch 4 *(counts as first dc and ch-1 sp)*, [dc in ring, ch 1] 11 times, join with sl st in 3rd ch of beg ch-4. *(12 ch sps)*

**Rnd 2:** Sl st across to first ch sp, ch 4 *(counts as first tr)*, tr in same ch sp, ch 2, [2 tr in next ch sp, ch 2] around, join with sl st in 4th ch of beg ch-4.

**Rnd 3:** Sl st across to first ch sp, ch 4, 2 tr in same ch sp, ch 3, [3 tr in next ch sp, ch 3] around, join with sl st in 4th ch of beg ch-4.

**Rnd 4:** Sl st across to first ch sp, ch 4, 3 tr in same ch sp, ch 4, [4 tr in next ch sp, ch 4] around, join with sl st in 4th ch of beg ch-4.

**Rnd 5:** Sl st across to first ch sp, ch 4, 4 tr in same ch sp, ch 5, [5 tr in next ch sp, ch 5] around, join with sl st in 4th ch of beg ch-4.

**Rnd 6:** Sl st across to first ch sp, ch 4, 5 tr in same ch sp, ch 6, [6 tr in next ch sp, ch 6] around, join with sl st in 4th ch of beg ch-4.

**Rnd 7:** Sl st in each of next 2 sts, ch 1, sc in next st, ch 3, *(sc, ch 5, sc) in next ch sp, ch 3**, sk next 3 sts, sc in next st, ch 3, rep from * around, ending last rep at **, join with sl st in beg sc.

**Rnd 8:** Ch 1, sc in first ch sp, *ch 3, 9 dc in next ch-5 sp, ch 3, sc in next ch sp, ch 2**, sc in next ch sp, rep from * around, ending last rep at **, join with sl st in beg sc.

**Rnd 9:** Sl st in each of next 3 chs, sl st in next st, ch 4 *(counts as first dc and ch-1 sp)*, *dc in next st, [ch 1, dc in next st] 7 times, ch 3, sk next ch sp, sc in next ch sp, ch 3, sk next ch sp**, dc in next st, ch 1, rep from * around, ending last rep at **, join with sl st in 3rd ch of beg ch-4.

**Rnd 10:** Ch 1, sc in first ch-1 sp, *[ch 2, sc in next ch-1 sp] 7 times, ch 5, sk next 2 ch sps**, sc in next ch-1 sp, rep from * around, ending last rep at **, join with sl st in beg sc.

**Rnd 11:** Ch 1, sc in first ch-2 sp, *[ch 2, sc in next ch-2 sp] 6 times, ch 6, sk next ch sp**, sc in next ch-2 sp, rep from * around, ending last rep at **, join with sl st in beg sc.

**Rnd 12:** Ch 1, sc in first ch-2 sp, *[ch 2, sc in next ch-2 sp] 5 times, ch 7, sk next ch sp**, sc in next ch-2 sp, rep from * around, ending last rep at **, join with sl st in beg sc.

**Rnd 13:** Ch 1, sc in first ch-2 sp, *[ch 2, sc in next ch-2 sp] 4 times, ch 8, sk next ch sp**, sc in next ch-2 sp, rep from * around, ending last rep at **, join with sl st in beg sc.

**Rnd 14:** Ch 1, sc in first ch-2 sp, *[ch 2, sc in next ch-2 sp] 3 times, ch 5, sc in next ch sp, ch 5**, sc in next ch-2 sp, rep from * around, ending last rep at **, join with sl st in beg sc.

**Rnd 15:** Ch 1, sc in first ch-2 sp, *[ch 2, sc in next ch-2 sp] twice, ch 5, sc in next ch sp, ch 4, sc in next ch sp, ch 5**, sc in next ch-2 sp, rep from * around, ending last rep at **, join with sl st in beg sc.

**Rnd 16:** Ch 1, sc in first ch-2 sp, *ch 2, sc in next ch-2 sp, ch 5, sc in next ch sp, ch 3, (tr, ch 2, tr) in next ch sp, ch 3, sc in next ch sp, ch 5**, sc in next ch-2 sp, rep from * around, ending last rep at **, join with sl st in beg sc.

**Rnd 17:** Ch 1, sc in first ch-2 sp, *ch 5, sc in next ch sp, ch 5, sk next ch sp, (2 tr, ch 2, 2 tr) in next ch sp, ch 5, sk next ch sp, sc in next ch sp, ch 5**, sc in next ch-2 sp, rep from * around, ending last rep at **, join with sl st in beg sc.

**Rnd 18:** Sl st in each of first 2 chs, ch 1, sc in same ch sp, ch 5, sc in next ch sp, ch 5, *({2 dc, ch 2} twice, 2 dc) in next ch sp**, ch 5, [sc in next ch sp, ch 5] 4 times, rep from * around, ending last rep at **, ch 5, [sc in next ch sp, ch 5] around, join with sl st in beg sc.

**Rnd 19:** Sl st in each of first 2 chs, ch 1, sc in same ch sp, ch 5, sc in next ch sp, ch 5, *(2 tr, ch 2, 2 tr) in next ch sp, ch 2, (2 tr, ch 2, 2 tr) in next ch sp, [ch 5, sc in next ch sp] twice, ch 5, (dc, ch 2, dc) in next ch sp**, [ch 5, sc in next ch sp] twice, ch 5, rep from * around, ending last rep at **, ch 5, join with sl st in beg sc.

**Rnd 20:** Ch 1, ({sc, ch 2} twice) in each ch sp around, join with sl st in beg sc. Fasten off.

# Spring Green

## SKILL LEVEL

INTERMEDIATE

## FINISHED SIZE
7 inches in diameter

## MATERIALS
- DMC Cebelia size 10 crochet cotton (282 yds per ball):
    1 ball #745 banana yellow
    1 ball #955 nile green
- Size 7/1.65mm steel hook or size needed to obtain gauge

## GAUGE
Rnds 1 and 2 = 1 inch in diameter

## INSTRUCTIONS

### DOILY

**Rnd 1:** With yellow, ch 6, sl st in first ch to form ring, ch 1, 12 sc in ring, join with sl st in beg sc. *(12 sc)*

**Rnd 2:** Ch 3 *(counts as first dc)*, dc in same st, 2 dc in each st around, join with sl st in 3rd ch of beg ch-3. *(24 dc)*

**Rnd 3:** Ch 3, dc in each of next 2 sts, ch 2, [dc in each of next 3 sts, ch 2] around, join with sl st in 3rd ch of beg ch-3.

**Rnd 4:** Ch 3, dc in each of next 2 sts, ch 3, [dc in each of next 3 sts, ch 3] around, join with sl st in 3rd ch of beg ch-3. Fasten off.

**Rnd 5:** Join green with sl st in first st, ch 3, dc in each of next 3 sts, *working in front of ch sp on last rnd, 3 tr in ch sp on rnd 3**, dc in each of next 3 sts, rep from * around, ending last rep at **, join with sl st in 3rd ch of beg ch-3.

**Rnd 6:** Sl st in each of next 3 sts, ch 3, dc in each of next 2 sts, *ch 6, sk next 3 sts**, dc in each of next 3 sts, rep from * around, ending last rep at **, join with sl st in 3rd ch of beg ch-3.

**Rnd 7:** Ch 3, dc in each of next 2 sts, *ch 4, dc in next ch sp, ch 4**, dc in each of next 3 sts, rep from * around, ending last rep at **, join with sl st in 3rd ch of beg ch-3.

**Rnd 8:** Ch 3, dc in each of next 2 sts, *ch 3, sc in next ch sp, ch 3, dc in next st, ch 3, sc in next ch sp, ch 3**, dc in each of next 3 sts, rep from * around, ending last rep at **, join with sl st in 3rd ch of beg ch-3.

**Rnd 9:** Ch 3, dc in each of next 2 sts, *[ch 3, sc in next ch sp] twice, ch 3, dc in next st, [ch 3, sc in next ch sp] twice, ch 3**, dc in each of next 3 sts, rep from * around, ending last rep at **, join with sl st in 3rd ch of beg ch-3.

**Rnd 10:** Ch 3, dc in each of next 2 sts, *ch 3, sk next 2 ch sps, (dc, ch 1, dc) in next ch sp, ch 1, dc in next st, ch 1, (dc, ch 1, dc) in next ch sp, ch 3, sk next 2 ch sps**, dc in each of next 3 sts, rep from * around, ending last rep at **, join with sl st in 3rd ch of beg ch-3.

**Rnd 11:** Ch 3, dc in each of next 2 sts, *ch 3, sk next ch sp, sc in next ch sp, ch 7, sk next 2 ch sps, sc in next ch sp, ch 3, sk next ch sp**, dc in each of next 3 sts, rep from * around, ending last rep at **, join with sl st in 3rd ch of beg ch-3.

**Rnd 12:** Ch 3, dc in each of next 2 sts, *ch 5, sk next ch sp, 9 dc in next ch sp, ch 5, sk next ch sp**, dc in each of next 3 sts, rep from * around, ending last rep at **, join with sl st in 3rd ch of beg ch-3.

**Rnd 13:** Ch 3, dc in each of next 2 sts, *ch 5, sk next ch sp, dc in next st, [ch 1, dc in next st] 8 times, ch 5, sk next ch sp**, dc in each of next 3 sts, rep from * around, ending last rep at **, join with sl st in 3rd ch of beg ch-3. Fasten off.

**Rnd 14:** Join yellow, with sc in first st, sc in each of next 2 sts, *ch 5, sk next ch sp, sc in next ch sp, [ch 2, sc in next ch sp] 7 times, ch 5, sk next ch sp**, sc in each of next 3 sts, rep from * around, ending last rep at **, join with sl st in beg sc.

**Rnd 15:** Ch 1, sc in each of first 3 sts, *ch 2, sc in next ch sp, ch 2, (sc, ch 3, sc) in each of next 7 ch sps, ch 2, sc in next ch sp, ch 2**, sc in each of next 3 sts, rep from * around, ending last rep at **, join with sl st in beg sc. Fasten off.

# Starflower

**SKILL LEVEL**

EASY

## FINISHED SIZE
8½ inches in diameter

## MATERIALS
- Size 10 crochet cotton:
    200 yds linen
- Size 7/1.65mm steel hook or size needed to obtain gauge

## GAUGE
Rnds 1 and 2 = 1¾ inches in diameter

## SPECIAL STITCHES

**2-treble crochet cluster (2-tr cl):** Holding last lp of each st on hook, 2 tr in next st or ch sp, yo, pull through all lps on hook.

**3-treble crochet cluster (3-tr cl):** Holding last lp of each st on hook, 3 tr in next st or ch sp, yo, pull through all lps on hook.

**Picot:** Ch 3, sl st in 3rd ch from hook.

## INSTRUCTIONS

### DOILY

**Rnd 1:** Ch 6, sl st in first ch to form ring, ch 1, (sc, ch 4, **2-tr cl**—*see Special Stitches*, ch 4, sc) 5 times in ring, join with sl st in beg sc. *(5 2-tr cls)*

**Rnd 2:** Sl st in each of next 4 chs, ch 1, sc in top of 2-tr cl, ch 5 *(counts as first tr and ch-1 sp)*, tr in same st, ch 8, [(tr, ch 1, tr) in top of next 2-tr cl, ch 8] around, join with sl st in 4th ch of beg ch-5.

**Rnd 3:** Sl st in next ch sp, ch 4, (tr, ch 2, 2 tr) in same ch sp, *ch 5, sc in next ch sp, ch 5**, (2 tr, ch 2, 2 tr) in next ch sp, rep from * around, ending last rep at **, join with sl st in 4th ch of beg ch-4.

**Rnd 4:** Sl st across to first ch sp, ch 4, (2 tr, ch 2, 3 tr) in same ch sp, *ch 4, [sc in next ch sp, ch 4] twice**, (3 tr, ch 2, 3 tr) in next ch sp, rep from * around, ending last rep at **, join with sl st in 4th ch of beg ch-4.

**Rnd 5:** Sl st across to first ch sp, ch 4, (2 tr, ch 2, 3 tr) in same ch sp, *ch 4, [sc in next ch sp, ch 4] 3 times**, (3 tr, ch 2, 3 tr) in next ch sp, rep from * around, ending last rep at **, join with sl st in 4th ch of beg ch-4.

**Rnd 6:** Sl st across to first ch sp, ch 4, (tr, {ch 2, 2 tr} twice) in same ch sp, *ch 4, sc in next ch sp, ch 4, **3-tr cl** *(see Special Stitches)* in next ch sp, ch 2, 3-tr cl in next ch sp, ch 4, sc in next ch sp, ch 4**, ({2 tr, ch 2} twice, 2 tr) in next ch sp, rep from * around, ending last rep at **, join with sl st in 4th ch of beg ch-4.

**Rnd 7:** Sl st across to first ch sp, ch 4, (2 tr, ch 2, 3 tr) in same ch sp, *ch 2, (3 tr, ch 2, 3 tr) in next ch sp, ch 4, sc in next ch sp, ch 4, 3-tr cl in next ch sp, [ch 2, 3-tr cl in next ch sp] twice, ch 4, sc in next ch sp, ch 4**, (3 tr, ch 2, 3 tr) in next ch sp, rep from * around, ending last rep at **, join with sl st in 4th ch of beg ch-4.

**Rnd 8:** Sl st across to first ch sp, ch 4, (tr, ch 2, 2 tr) in same ch sp, *ch 2, (tr, ch 1, tr) in next ch sp, ch 2, (2 tr, ch 2, 2 tr) in next ch sp, ch 4, sc in next ch sp, ch 4, 3-tr cl in next ch sp, [ch 2, 3-tr cl in next ch sp] 3 times, ch 4, sc in next ch sp, ch 4**, (2 tr, ch 2, 2 tr) in next ch sp, rep from * around, ending last rep at **, join with sl st in 4th ch of beg ch-4.

**Rnd 9:** Sl st across to first ch sp, ch 4, (2 tr, ch 2, 3 tr) in same ch sp, *ch 2, sk next ch sp, (tr, ch 1, tr) in next ch sp, ch 2, sk next ch sp, (3 tr, ch 2, 3 tr) in next ch sp, [ch 4, sc in next ch sp] twice, ch 4, 3-tr cl in next ch sp, [ch 2, 3-tr cl in next ch sp] twice, [ch 4, sc in next ch sp] twice, ch 4**, (3 tr, ch 2, 3 tr) in next ch sp, rep from * around, ending last rep at **, join with sl st in 4th ch of beg ch-4.

**Rnd 10:** Sl st across to first ch sp, ch 4, (tr, {ch 2, 2 tr} twice) in same ch sp, ch 4, sk next ch sp, (2 tr, ch 2, 2 tr) in next ch sp, ch 4, sk next ch sp, ({2 tr, ch 2} twice, 2 tr) in next ch sp, [ch 4, sc in next ch sp] 3 times, ch 4, 3-tr cl in next ch sp, ch 2, 3-tr cl in next ch sp, [ch 4, sc in next ch sp] 3 times, ch 4**, ({2 tr, ch 2} twice, 2 tr) in next ch sp, rep from * around, ending last rep at **, join with sl st in 4th ch of beg ch-4.

**Rnd 11:** Sl st across to first ch sp, (sc, **picot**—*see Special Stitches*, ch 3) in first ch sp and in each ch-2 sp around, with (sc, picot, sc, ch 3) in each ch-4 sp, join with sl st in beg sc. Fasten off.

# Blue Skies

## SKILL LEVEL

EASY

## FINISHED SIZE
9½ inches square

## MATERIALS
- DMC Cebelia size 10 crochet cotton (282 yds per ball):
    1 ball #747 sea mist blue
- Size 7/1.65mm steel hook or size needed to obtain gauge

## GAUGE
Rnd 1 = 1 inch in diameter

## INSTRUCTIONS

## DOILY

**Rnd 1:** Ch 6, sl st in first ch to form ring, ch 4 *(counts as first tr)*, 19 tr in ring, join with sl st in 4th ch of beg ch-4. *(20 tr)*

**Rnd 2:** Ch 6 *(counts as first tr and ch-2 sp)*, tr in same st, ch 9, sk next 4 sts, [(tr, ch 2, tr) in next st, ch 9, sk next 4 sts] around, join with sl st in 4th ch of beg ch-6.

**Rnd 3:** Sl st in first ch sp, ch 4, (tr, ch 2, 2 tr) in same ch sp, *ch 6, (sc, ch 3, sc) in next ch sp, ch 6**, (2 tr, ch 2, 2 tr) in next ch sp, rep from * around, ending last rep at **, join with sl st in 4th ch of beg ch-4.

**Rnd 4:** Sl st across to first ch sp, ch 4, (tr, ch 2, 2 tr) in same ch sp, *ch 4, sc in next ch sp, ch 8, sk next ch sp, sc in next ch sp, ch 4**, (2 tr, ch 2, 2 tr) in next ch sp, rep from * around, ending last rep at **, join with sl st in 4th ch of beg ch-4.

**Rnd 5:** Sl st across to first ch sp, ch 4, (2 tr, ch 2, 3 tr) in same ch sp, *ch 4, (sc, ch 4, sc) in next ch sp, ch 4, (tr, ch 2, tr) in next ch sp, ch 4, (sc, ch 4, sc) in next ch sp, ch 4**, (3 tr, ch 2, 3 tr) in next ch sp, rep from * around, ending last rep at **, join with sl st in 4th ch of beg ch-4.

**Rnd 6:** Sl st across to first ch sp, ch 4, (2 tr, ch 2, 3 tr) in same ch sp, *ch 4, sc in next ch sp, ch 6, sk next ch sp, sc in next ch sp, ch 4, (2 tr, ch 2, 2 tr) in next ch sp, ch 4, sc in next ch sp, ch 6, sk next ch sp, sc in next ch sp, ch 4**, (3 tr, ch 2, 3 tr) in next ch sp, rep from * around, ending last rep at **, join with sl st in 4th ch of beg ch-4.

**Rnd 7:** Sl st across to first ch sp, ch 4, (2 tr, ch 2, 3 tr) in same ch sp, *ch 4, (sc, ch 4, sc) in next ch sp, ch 4, sc in next ch sp, ch 4, sk next ch sp, ({tr, ch 1} 3 times, tr) in next ch sp, ch 4, sk next ch sp, sc in next ch sp, ch 4, (sc, ch 4, sc) in next ch sp, ch 4**, (3 tr, ch 2, 3 tr) in next ch sp, rep from * around, ending last rep at **, join with sl st in 4th ch of beg ch-4.

**Rnd 8:** Sl st across to first ch sp, ch 4, (2 tr, ch 2, 3 tr) in same ch sp, *ch 4, [(sc, ch 4, sc) in next ch sp, ch 4, sk next ch sp] twice, tr in next tr, [ch 1, tr in next ch sp, ch 1, tr in next st] 3 times, [ch 4, sk next ch sp, (sc, ch 4, sc)] twice, ch 4**, (3 tr, ch 2, 3 tr) in next ch sp, rep from * around, ending last rep at **, join with sl st in 4th ch of beg ch-4.

**Rnd 9:** Sl st across to first ch sp, ch 4, (2 tr, ch 2, 3 tr) in same ch sp, *ch 4, (sc, ch 4, sc) in next ch sp, ch 4, sk next ch sp, (sc, ch 4, sc) in next ch sp, ch 6, sk next 2 ch sps, tr in next tr, [ch 2, tr in next st] 6 times, ch 6, sk next 2 ch sps, (sc, ch 4, sc) in next ch sp, ch 4, sk next ch sp, (sc, ch 4, sc) in next ch sp, ch 4 **, (3 tr, ch 2, 3 tr) in next ch sp, rep from * around, ending last rep at **, join with sl st in 4th ch of beg ch-4.

**Rnd 10:** Sl st across to first ch sp, ch 4, (2 tr, ch 2, 3 tr) in same ch sp, *ch 4, (sc, ch 4, sc) in next ch sp, ch 4, sk next ch sp, (sc, ch 4, sc) in next ch sp, ch 7, sk next 2 ch sps, tr in next tr, [ch 3, tr in next st] 6 times, ch 7, sk next 2 ch sps, (sc, ch 4, sc) in next ch sp, ch 4, sk next ch sp, (sc, ch 4, sc) in next ch sp, ch 4**, (3 tr, ch 2, 3 tr) in next ch sp, rep from * around, ending last rep at **, join with sl st in 4th ch of beg ch-4.

**Rnd 11:** Sl st across to first ch sp, ch 4, (2 tr, ch 4, sl st in 3rd ch from hook, ch 1, 3 tr) in same ch sp, *ch 5, (sc, ch 4, sc) in next ch sp, ch 6, sk next ch sp, (sc, ch 4, sc) in next ch sp, ch 10, sk next 2 ch sps, tr in next tr, [ch 5, sl st in 3rd ch from hook, ch 2, tr in next st] 6 times, ch 10, sk next 2 ch sps, (sc, ch 4, sc) in next ch sp, ch 6, sk next ch sp, (sc, ch 4, sc) in next ch sp, ch 5**, (3 tr, ch 4, sl st in 3rd ch from hook, ch 1, 3 tr) in next ch sp, rep from * around, ending last rep at **, join with sl st in 4th ch of beg ch-4. Fasten off.

# Sweetheart

## SKILL LEVEL

INTERMEDIATE

## FINISHED SIZE
11 inches in diameter

## MATERIALS
- Aunt Lydia's Classic size 10 crochet cotton:
    400 yds #1 white
    350 yds #484 victory red
- Size 6/1.80mm steel hook or size needed to obtain gauge

## GAUGE
Rnds 1–3 = 1½ inches in diameter

## SPECIAL STITCHES

**Cluster (cl):** Holding last lp of each st on hook, 2 tr in next st, yo, pull through all lps on hook.

**Picot:** Ch 5, sl st in 3rd ch from hook.

**Motif joining (join):** [Ch 2, sc in corresponding picot on last Motif, ch 2, sc in next ch sp on this Motif] twice.

## INSTRUCTIONS

### DOILY

**Center**

**Rnd 1:** With white, ch 5, sl st in first ch to form ring, ch 3 *(counts as first dc)*, 15 dc in ring, join with sl st in 3rd ch of beg ch-3. *(16 dc)*

**Rnd 2:** Ch 3, dc in same st, ch 2, sk next st, [2 dc in next st, ch 2, sk next sp] around, join with sl st in 3rd ch of beg ch-3.

**Rnd 3:** Ch 3, dc in same st, dc in next st, ch 3, sk next ch sp, [2 dc in next st, dc in next st, ch 3, sk next sp] around, join with sl st in 3rd ch of beg ch-3.

**Rnd 4:** Ch 3, dc in same st, *dc in each of next 2 sts, ch 4, sk next ch sp**, 2 dc in next st, rep from * around, ending last rep at **, join with sl st in 3rd ch of beg ch-3.

**Rnd 5:** Ch 3, dc in same st, *dc in each of next 3 sts, ch 5, sk next ch sp**, 2 dc in next st, rep from * around, ending last rep at **, join with sl st in 3rd ch of beg ch-3.

**Rnd 6:** Ch 3, dc in same st, *dc in each of next 4 sts, ch 6, sk next ch sp**, 2 dc in next st, rep from * around, ending last rep at **, join with sl st in 3rd ch of beg ch-3.

**Rnd 7:** Ch 3, dc in each of next 2 sts, *ch 2, dc in each of next 3 sts, ch 4, sc in next ch sp, ch 4**, dc in each of next 3 sts, rep from * around, ending last rep at **, join with sl st in 3rd ch of beg ch-3.

**Rnd 8:** Ch 3, dc in each of next 2 sts, *ch 3, sk next ch sp, dc in each of next 3 sts, [ch 4, sc in next ch sp] twice, ch 4**, dc in each of next 3 sts, rep from * around, ending last rep at **, join with sl st in 3rd ch of beg ch-3.

**Rnd 9:** Ch 3, dc in each of next 2 sts, *ch 4, sk next ch sp, dc in each of next 3 sts, [ch 4, sc in next ch sp] 3 times, ch 4**, dc in each of next 3 sts, rep from * around, ending last rep at **, join with sl st in 3rd ch of beg ch-3.

**Rnd 10:** Ch 3, dc in each of next 2 sts, *ch 3, sc in next ch sp, ch 3, dc in each of next 3 sts, [ch 3, sc in next ch sp] 4 times, ch 3**, dc in each of next 3 sts, rep from * around, ending last rep at **, join with sl st in 3rd ch of beg ch-3. Fasten off.

## First Motif

**Rnd 1:** With victory red, ch 5, sl st in first ch to form ring, ch 1, 14 sc in ring, join with sl st in beg sc. *(14 sc)*

**Rnd 2:** Ch 1, sc in first st, *ch 3, **cl** *(see Special Stitches)* in next st, ch 3**, sc in next st, rep from * around, ending last rep at **, join with sl st in beg sc. Fasten off.

**Rnd 3:** Join white with sl st in top of any cl, ch 3, (dc, ch 2, 2 dc) in same st, ch 3, [(2 dc, ch 3, 2 dc) in next cl, ch 3] around, join with sl st in 3rd ch of beg ch-3.

**Rnd 4:** Sl st across to first ch sp, ch 3, (2 dc, ch 2, 3 dc) in same ch sp, *ch 3, sc in next ch sp, ch 3**, (3 dc, ch 2, 3 dc) in next ch sp, rep from * around, ending last rep at **, join with sl st in 3rd ch of beg ch-3.

**Rnd 5:** Sl st across to first ch sp, ch 1, sc in same ch sp, ***picot** *(see Special Stitches)*, [ch 3, sc in next ch sp] twice, picot, ch 3**, sc in next ch sp, rep from * 5 times, ending last rep at **, holding Motif to RS of Center matching groups of dc, working through both thicknesses, sc in next ch sp, [ch 3, sc in next ch sp] twice, ch 3, sl st in next ch sp on Center, join with sl st in beg sc on Motif. Fasten off.

## Next Motif

**Rnds 1–4:** Rep rnds 1–4 of First Motif.

**Rnd 5:** Sl st across to first ch sp, ch 1, sc in same ch sp, picot, [ch 3, sc in next ch sp] twice, **join** *(see Special Stitches)*, ch 3, *[sc in next ch sp, picot, ch 3]** twice, ch 3, rep from * around, ending last rep at **, holding Motif to WS of Center matching groups of dc, working through both thicknesses, sc in next ch sp, [ch 3, sc in next ch sp] twice, ch 3, sl st in next ch sp on Center, join with sl st in beg sc. Fasten off.

Rep Next Motif around until 8 Motifs are completed; join last Motif to First Motif.

# Mint Julep

## SKILL LEVEL
INTERMEDIATE

## FINISHED SIZE
8½ inches square

## MATERIALS
- Aunt Lydia's size 10 crochet cotton:
    150 yds #428 mint green
- Size 7/1.65mm steel crochet hook or size needed to obtain gauge

## GAUGE

Rnds 1 and 2 = 1½ inches across

## SPECIAL STITCHES

**Small shell (sm shell):** (2 tr, ch 2, 2 tr) in next st or ch sp.

**Large shell (lg shell):** (3 tr, ch 2, 3 tr) in next st or ch sp.

## INSTRUCTIONS

### DOILY

**Rnd 1:** Ch 6, sl st in first ch to form ring, ch 1, 12 sc in ring, join with sl st in beg sc. *(12 sc)*

**Rnd 2:** Ch 4 *(counts as first tr)*, tr in same st, 2 tr in each of next 2 sts, ch 3, [2 tr in each of next 3 sts, ch 3] around, join with sl st in 4th ch of beg ch-4. *(24 tr, 4 ch-3 sps)*

**Rnd 3:** Ch 4 tr in next st, *ch 2, sk next 2 sts, tr in each of next 2 sts, (dc, ch 3, dc) in next corner ch sp**, tr in each of next 2 sts, rep from * around, ending last rep at **, join with sl st in 4th ch of beg ch-4.

**Rnd 4:** Ch 5 *(counts as first tr and ch-1)*, *(tr, ch 2, tr) in next ch sp, ch 1, sk next st, tr in next st, ch 2, sk next st, (sc, ch 5, sc) in next corner ch sp, ch 2, sk next st**, tr in next st, ch 1, rep from * around, ending last rep at **, join with sl st in 4th ch of beg ch-5.

**Rnd 5:** Ch 5, *sm shell *(see Special Stitches)* in next ch-2 sp, ch 1, sk next st, tr in next st, ch 2, 7 tr in next corner ch-5 sp, ch 2, sk next st**, tr in next st, ch 1, rep from * around, ending last rep at **, join with sl st in 4th ch of beg ch-5.

**Rnd 6:** Ch 6 *(counts as first tr and ch-2 sp)*, *sm shell in ch sp of next sm shell, ch 2, sk next 2 sts, tr in next st, ch 4, tr in next st, [ch 1, tr in next st] 6 times, ch 4**, tr in next st, ch 2, rep from * around, ending last rep at **, join with sl st in 4th ch of beg ch-6.

**Rnd 7:** Ch 6, *lg shell *(see Special Stitches)* in ch sp of next sm shell, ch 2, sk next 2 sts, tr in next st, ch 4, sk next ch sp, sc in next ch-1 sp, [ch 3, sc in next ch-1 sp] 5 times, ch 4, sk next ch sp**, tr in next st, ch 2, rep from * around, ending last rep at **, join with sl st in 4th ch of beg ch-6.

**Rnd 8:** Ch 5, tr in same st, *ch 1, lg shell in ch sp of next lg shell, ch 1, sk next 3 sts, (tr, ch 1, tr) in next st, ch 4, sk next ch sp, sc in next ch-3 sp, [ch 3, sc in next ch-3 sp] 4 times, ch 4, sk next ch-4 sp**, (tr ch 1, tr) in next st, rep from * around, ending last rep at **, join with sl st in 4th ch of beg ch-5.

**Rnd 9:** Sl st in first ch sp, ch 5, (tr, ch 1, tr) in same ch sp, *ch 3, sk next ch sp (2 tr, ch 2, 2 tr, ch 2, 2 tr) in ch sp of next lg shell, ch 3, sk next ch sp, (tr, ch 1, tr, ch 1, tr) in next ch sp, ch 4, sk next ch sp, sc in next ch-3 sp, [ch 3, sc in next ch-3 sp] 3 times, ch 4, sk next ch sp**, (tr, ch 1, tr, ch 1, tr) in next ch sp, rep from * around, ending last rep at **, join with sl st in 4th ch of beg ch-5.

**Rnd 10:** Sl st in first ch-1 sp, ch 5, tr in same ch sp, *ch 1, (tr, ch 1, tr) in next ch-1 sp, ch 3, sk next ch sp, lg shell in each of next 2 ch-2 sps, ch 3, sk next ch sp, (tr, ch 1, tr) in next ch-1 sp, ch 1, (tr, ch 1, tr) in next ch-1 sp, ch 4, sk next ch sp, sc in next ch-3 sp, [ch 3, sc in next ch-3 sp] twice, ch 4, sk next ch sp**, (tr, ch 1, tr) in next ch-1 sp, rep from * around, ending last rep at **, join with sl st in 4th ch of beg ch-5.

**Rnd 11:** Sl st in first ch sp, ch 5, tr in same ch sp, *(ch 1, tr, ch 1, tr) in each of next 2 ch sps, ch 3, lg shell in ch sp of next lg shell, ch 1, 2 tr in sp between lg shells, ch 1, lg shell in ch sp of next lg shell, ch 3, [(tr, ch 1, tr) in next ch sp, ch 1] twice, (tr, ch 1, tr) in next ch sp, ch 4, sk next ch sp, sc in next ch-3 sp, ch 3, sc in next ch sp, ch 4, sk next ch sp**, (tr, ch 1, tr) in next ch sp, rep from * around, ending last rep at **, join with sl st in 4th ch of beg ch-5.

**Rnd 12:** Sl st in next ch sp, ch 5, tr in same ch sp, *[ch 1, (tr, ch 1, tr) in next ch sp] 4 times, ch 3, sk next ch sp, lg shell in ch sp of next lg shell, [ch 1, 2 tr in next ch sp] twice, ch 1, lg shell in ch sp of next lg shell, ch 3, sk next ch sp, [(tr, ch 1, tr) in next ch sp, ch 1] 4 times, (tr, ch 1, tr) in next ch sp, ch 3, sk next ch sp, sc in next ch-3 sp, ch 3, sk next ch sp**, (tr, ch 1, tr) in next ch sp, rep from * around, ending last rep at **, join with sl st in 4th ch of beg ch-5.

**Rnd 13:** Sl st in first ch sp, ch 1, sc in same ch sp, *[ch 3, sc in next ch sp] 8 times, ch 3, sk next ch sp, lg shell in ch sp of next lg shell, ch 3, sc in next ch sp, ch 2, (sc, ch 5, sc) in next ch sp, ch 2, sc in next ch sp, ch 3, lg shell in ch sp of next lg shell, ch 3, sk next ch sp, [sc in next ch sp, ch 3] 9 times, sk next 2 ch sps**, sc in next ch sp, rep from * around, ending last rep at **, join with sl st in beg sc.

**Rnd 14:** Sl st in first ch sp, ch 1, sc in same ch sp, *[ch 3, sc in next ch sp] 7 times, ch 3, lg shell in ch sp of next lg shell, ch 3, sc in next ch sp, ch 2, 9 tr in next ch-5 sp, ch 2, sk next ch sp, sc in next ch sp, ch 3, lg shell in next lg shell, ch 3, sk next ch sp, [sc in next ch sp, ch 3] 7 times, ch 1, sk next ch sp, sc in next ch sp, ch 1**, sc in next ch sp, rep from * around, ending last rep at **, join with sl st in beg sc.

**Rnd 15:** Sl st in first ch sp, ch 1, sc in same ch sp, ch 2, sc in same ch sp, (sc, ch 2, sc) in each of next 7 ch sps, *ch 2, sc in next ch sp, ch 4, (sc, ch 2, sc) in ch sp of next lg shell, ch 4, sc in next ch sp, [ch 2, sc in next ch sp, ch 2, sc in next st] 9 times, ch 2, sc in next ch sp, ch 4, (sc, ch 2, sc) in ch sp of next lg shell, ch 4, sc in next ch sp, ch 2, (sc, ch 2, sc) in each of next 7 ch sps, ch 2**, (sc, ch 2, sc) in each of next 7 ch sps, rep from * around, ending last rep at **, join with sl st in beg sc. Fasten off.

# Starburst

## SKILL LEVEL
INTERMEDIATE

## FINISHED SIZE
11½ inches in diameter

## MATERIALS
- Size 10 crochet cotton:
    300 yds linen
- Size 7/1.65mm steel hook or size needed to obtain gauge

## GAUGE
Rnd 1 = 1 inch in diameter

## SPECIAL STITCH

**Cluster (cl):** Holding last lp of each st on hook, 3 tr in next ch sp, yo, pull through all lps on hook.

## INSTRUCTIONS

### DOILY

**Rnd 1:** Ch 6, sl st in first ch to form ring, ch 4 *(counts as first tr)*, 23 tr in ring, join with sl st in 4th ch of beg ch-4. *(24 tr)*

**Rnd 2:** Ch 8 *(counts as first tr and ch-4 sp)*, sk next st, [tr in next st, ch 4, sk next st] around, join with sl st in 4th ch of beg ch-4.

**Rnd 3:** Sl st in first ch sp, ch 4, (tr, ch 2, 2 tr) in same ch sp, *ch 4, sc in next ch sp, ch 4**, (2 tr, ch 2, 2 tr) in next ch sp, rep from * around, ending last rep at **, join with sl st in 4th ch of beg ch-4.

**Rnd 4:** Sl st across to first ch sp, ch 4, (tr, ch 2, 2 tr) in same ch sp, *ch 4, sc in next ch sp, ch 3, sc in next ch sp, ch 4**, (2 tr, ch 2, 2 tr) in next ch sp, rep from * around, ending last rep at **, join with sl st in 4th ch of beg ch-4.

**Rnd 5:** Sl st across to first ch sp, ch 4, (tr, ch 2, 2 tr) in first ch sp, * [ch 4, sc in next ch sp] 3 times, ch 4**, (2 tr, ch 2, 2 tr) in next ch sp, rep from * around, ending last rep at **, join with sl st in 4th ch of beg ch-4.

**Rnd 6:** Sl st across to first ch sp, ch 4, (tr, ch 2, 2 tr) in next ch sp, *ch 4, sc in next ch sp, ch 4, **cl** *(see Special Stitch)* in next ch sp, ch 2, cl in next ch sp, ch 4, sc in next ch sp, ch 4**, (2 tr, ch 2, 2 tr) in next ch sp, rep from * around, ending last rep at **, join with sl st in 4th ch of beg ch-4.

**Rnd 7:** Sl st across to first ch sp, ch 4, (tr, ch 2, 2 tr) in same ch sp, *ch 4, sc in next ch sp, ch 4, [cl in next ch sp, ch 2] twice, cl in next ch sp, ch 4, sc in next ch sp, ch 4**, (2 tr, ch 2, 2 tr) in next ch sp, rep from * around, ending last rep at **, join with sl st in 4th ch of beg ch-4.

**Rnd 8:** Sl st across to first ch sp, ch 4, (2 tr, ch 2, 3 tr) in same ch sp, *[ch 4, sc in next ch sp] twice, ch 4, cl in next ch sp, ch 2, cl in next ch sp, ch 4, [sc in next ch sp, ch 4] twice**, (3 tr, ch 2, 3 tr) in next ch sp, rep from * around, ending last rep at **, join with sl st in 4th ch of beg ch-4.

**Rnd 9:** Sl st across to first ch sp, ch 4, (2 tr, ch 2, 3 tr) in same ch sp, *[ch 4, sc in next ch sp] twice, ch 4, [cl in next ch sp, ch 2] twice, cl in next ch sp, ch 4, [sc in next ch sp, ch 4] twice**, (3 tr, ch 2, 3 tr) in next ch sp, rep from * around, ending last rep at **, join with sl st in 4th ch of beg ch-4.

**Rnd 10:** Sl st across to first ch sp, ch 4, (2 tr, ch 2, 3 tr) in same ch sp, *[ch 4, sc in next ch sp] 3 times, ch 4, cl in next ch sp, ch 2, cl in next ch sp, ch 4, [sc in next ch sp, ch 4] 3 times**, (3 tr, ch 2, 3 tr) in next ch sp, rep from * around, ending last rep at **, join with sl st in 4th ch of beg ch-4.

**Rnd 11:** Sl st across to first ch sp, ch 4, (2 tr, ch 2, 3 tr) in same ch sp, *[ch 4, sc in next ch sp] 4 times, ch 4, (sc, ch 6, sc) in next ch sp, ch 4, [sc in next ch sp, ch 4] 4 times**, (3 tr, ch 2, 3 tr) in next ch sp, rep from * around, ending last rep at **, join with sl st in 4th ch of beg ch-4.

**Rnd 12:** Sl st across to first ch sp, ch 4, (2 tr, ch 2, 3 tr) in same ch sp, *[ch 4, sc in next ch sp] 4 times, ch 4, sk next ch sp, 9 sc in next ch-6 sp, ch 4, sk next ch sp, [sc in next ch sp, ch 4] 4 times**, (3 tr, ch 2, 3 tr) in next ch sp, rep from * around, ending last rep at **, join with sl st in 4th ch of beg ch-4.

**Rnd 13:** Sl st across to first ch sp, ch 5 *(counts as first tr and ch-1 sp),* tr in same ch sp, (ch 1, tr) 5 times in same ch sp, *[ch 4, sc in next ch sp] 4 times, ch 4, sk next ch sp, tr in next st, (ch 1, tr) in each of next 8 sts, ch 4, sk next ch sp, [sc in next ch sp, ch 4] 4 times**, tr in next ch sp, (ch 1, tr) 6 times in same ch sp, rep from * around, ending last rep at **, join with sl st in 4th ch of beg ch-5.

**Rnd 14:** Sl st in first ch sp, ch 5, tr in same ch sp, *ch 2, (tr, ch 1, tr, ch 2) in each of next 4 ch sps, (tr, ch 1, tr) in next ch sp, ch 4, sk next ch sp, [sc in next ch sp, ch 4] 3 times, sk next ch sp, sc in next ch sp, [ch 2, sc in next ch sp] 7 times, ch 4, sk next ch sp, [sc in next ch sp, ch 4] 3 times**, (tr, ch 1, tr) in next ch sp, rep from * around, ending last rep at **, join with sl st in 4th ch of beg ch-5.

**Rnd 15:** Sl st in first ch sp, ch 5, tr in same ch sp, *ch 2, (tr, ch 1, tr, ch 2) in each of next 9 ch sps, (tr, ch 1, tr) in next ch sp, [ch 4, sc in next ch sp] 3 times, ch 6, sk next ch sp, (sc, ch 3, sc) in each of next 7 ch sps, ch 6, sk next ch sp, [sc in next ch sp, ch 4] 3 times**, (tr, ch 1, tr) in next ch sp, rep from * around, ending last rep at **, join with sl st in 4th ch of beg ch-5.

# STITCH GUIDE

## STITCH ABBREVIATIONS

| | |
|---|---|
| **beg** | begin/begins/beginning |
| **bpdc** | back post double crochet |
| **bpsc** | back post single crochet |
| **bptr** | back post treble crochet |
| **CC** | contrasting color |
| **ch(s)** | chain(s) |
| **ch-** | refers to chain or space previously made (i.e., ch-1 space) |
| **ch sp(s)** | chain space(s) |
| **cl(s)** | cluster(s) |
| **cm** | centimeter(s) |
| **dc** | double crochet (singular/plural) |
| **dc dec** | double crochet 2 or more stitches together, as indicated |
| **dec** | decrease/decreases/decreasing |
| **dtr** | double treble crochet |
| **ext** | extended |
| **fpdc** | front post double crochet |
| **fpsc** | front post single crochet |
| **fptr** | front post treble crochet |
| **g** | gram(s) |
| **hdc** | half double crochet |
| **hdc dec** | half double crochet 2 or more stitches together, as indicated |
| **inc** | increase/increases/increasing |
| **lp(s)** | loop(s) |
| **MC** | main color |
| **mm** | millimeter(s) |
| **oz** | ounce(s) |
| **pc** | popcorn(s) |
| **rem** | remain/remains/remaining |
| **rep(s)** | repeat(s) |
| **rnd(s)** | round(s) |
| **RS** | right side |
| **sc** | single crochet (singular/plural) |

| | |
|---|---|
| **sc dec** | single crochet 2 or more stitches together, as indicated |
| **sk** | skip/skipped/skipping |
| **sl st(s)** | slip stitch(es) |
| **sp(s)** | space(s)/spaced |
| **st(s)** | stitch(es) |
| **tog** | together |
| **tr** | treble crochet |
| **trtr** | triple treble |
| **WS** | wrong side |
| **yd(s)** | yard(s) |
| **yo** | yarn over |

## YARN CONVERSION
## OUNCES TO GRAMS

| | |
|---|---|
| 1 | 28.4 |
| 2 | 56.7 |
| 3 | 85.0 |
| 4 | 113.4 |

## GRAMS TO OUNCES

| | |
|---|---|
| 25 | 7/8 |
| 40 | 1 2/3 |
| 50 | 1 3/4 |
| 100 | 3 1/2 |

| UNITED STATES | | UNITED KINGDOM |
|---|---|---|
| sl st (slip stitch) | = | sc (single crochet) |
| sc (single crochet) | = | dc (double crochet) |
| hdc (half double crochet) | = | htr (half treble crochet) |
| dc (double crochet) | = | tr (treble crochet) |
| tr (treble crochet) | = | dtr (double treble crochet) |
| dtr (double treble crochet) | = | ttr (triple treble crochet) |
| skip | = | miss |

**Single crochet decrease (sc dec):** (Insert hook, yo, draw lp through) in each of the sts indicated, yo, draw through all lps on hook.

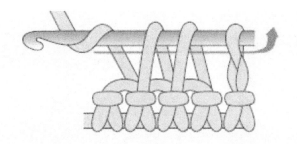

Example of 2-sc dec

**Half double crochet decrease (hdc dec):** (Yo, insert hook, yo, draw lp through) in each of the sts indicated, yo, draw through all lps on hook.

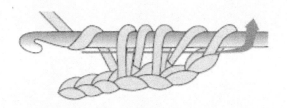

Example of 2-hdc dec

**Reverse single crochet (reverse sc):** Ch 1, sk first st, working from left to right, insert hook in next st from front to back, draw up lp on hook, yo and draw through both lps on hook.

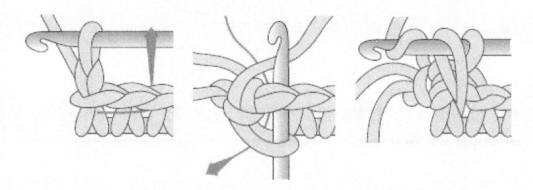

**Chain (ch):** Yo, pull through lp on hook.

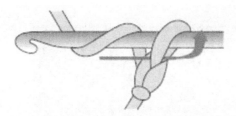

**Single crochet (sc):** Insert hook in st, yo, pull through st, yo, pull through both lps on hook.

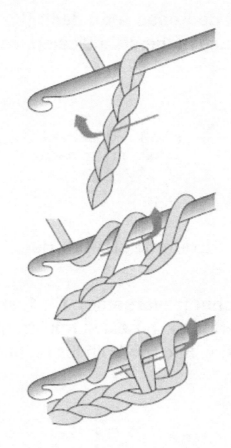

**Double crochet (dc):** Yo, insert hook in st, yo, pull through st, [yo, pull through 2 lps] twice.

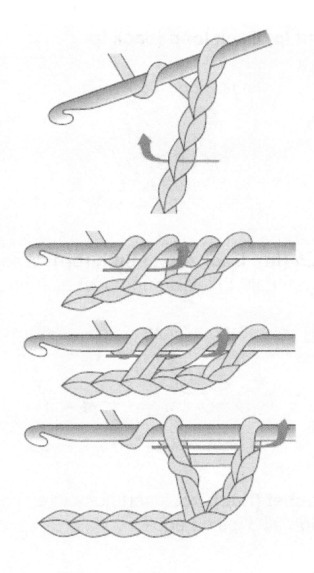

**Double crochet decrease (dc dec):** (Yo, insert hook, yo, draw lp through, yo, draw through 2 lps on hook) in each of the sts indicated, yo, draw through all lps on hook.

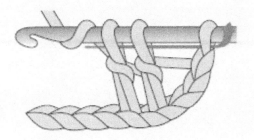

Example of 2-dc dec

**Front loop (front lp) Back loop (back lp)**

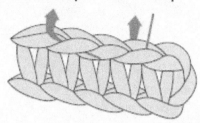

**Front post stitch (fp): Back post stitch (bp):** When working post st, insert hook from right to left around post of st on previous row.

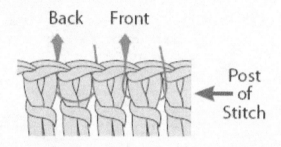

**Half double crochet (hdc):** Yo, insert hook in st, yo, pull through st, yo, pull through all 3 lps on hook.

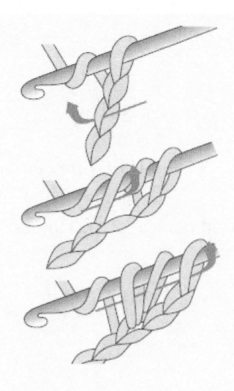

**Double treble crochet (dtr):** Yo 3 times, insert hook in st, yo, pull through st, [yo, pull through 2 lps] 4 times.

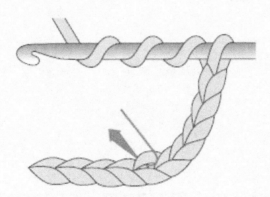

**Treble crochet decrease (tr dec):** Holding back last lp of each st, tr in each of the sts indicated, yo, pull through all lps on hook.

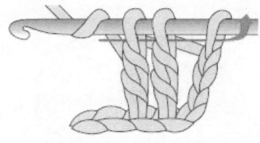

Example of 2-tr dec

**Slip stitch (sl st):** Insert hook in st, pull through both lps on hook.

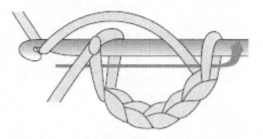

**Chain color change (ch color change)** Yo with new color, draw through last lp on hook.

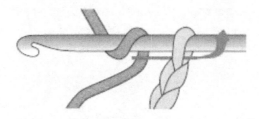

**Double crochet color change (dc color change)** Drop first color, yo with new color, draw through last 2 lps of st.

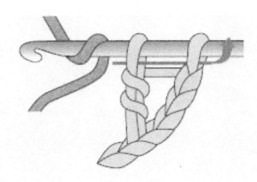

**Treble crochet (tr):** Yo twice, insert hook in st, yo, pull through st, [yo, pull through 2 lps] 3 times.

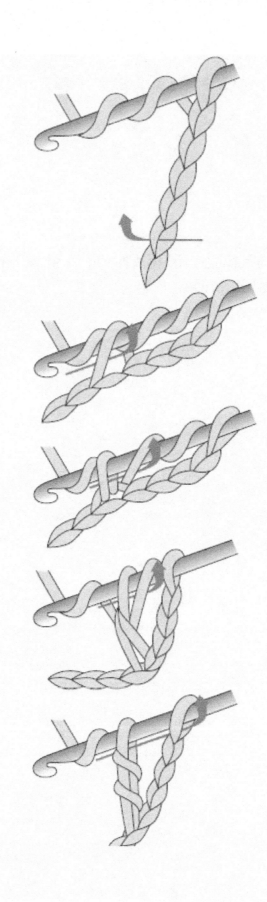

Made in the USA
Monee, IL
29 January 2025

11190132R00057